BARING MY SOUL
A journey of faith

Julie Roberts

Visit us online at www.authorsonline.co.uk

A Bright Pen Book

Copyright © Authors OnLine Ltd 2004

Text Copyright © Julie Roberts 2004

Cover design by James Fitt from an original painting by
Jenny Baker ©

All rights reserved. No part of this publication may be reproduced, stored in a retrieval system, or transmitted in any form or by any means, electronic, mechanical, photocopy, recording or otherwise, without prior written permission of the copyright owner. Nor can it be circulated in any form of binding or cover other than that in which it is published and without similar condition including this condition being imposed on a subsequent purchaser.

ISBN 0 7552 1010 7

Authors OnLine Ltd
40 Castle Street
Hertford SG14 1HR
England

This book is also available in e-book format, details of which are available at www.authorsonline.co.uk

In memory of Jonathan
In life my pride and joy
In death my inspiration

Acknowledgements

My sincere thanks to everyone
who has touched my life over the past five years
with their love, kindness, support, guidance, and encouragement,
but especially to my husband, John.

Over the last five years I have got to know the real me.
In Baring My Soul you will get to know me too.

Contents

Preface			1
One	–	An Ordinary Life	3
Two	–	The Peace That Passes All Understanding	6
Three	–	Simply Beyond Co-incidence	13
Four	–	A Life Changing Weekend	17
Five	–	An Unexpected Path Appears	22
Six	–	Life Journey And Spiritual Journey Meet	28
Seven	–	Listening	34
Eight	–	Getting To Grips With Prayer	40
Nine	–	On A Spiritual 'Fast Track'	46
Ten	–	Expecting The Unexpected	54
Eleven	–	Monday 24th March 2003	59

Twelve	–	God So Loved The World	64
Thirteen	–	The Way Things Were Meant To Be	69
Fourteen	–	'The Best Times Of My Life'	72
Fifteen	–	The Final Goodbye	77
Sixteen	–	As Free As A Bird	82
Seventeen	–	A Message From The Lord	86
Eighteen	–	Closing Thoughts	90
Nineteen	–	One Year On	97
Bibliography			100

Preface

There is nothing that could be taken from a parent more precious than a child, and now that this has happened to me, I feel it does not matter what people might say about the testimony that I am going to write. I have always sensed that when I talked about my plans people thought I was off on another mad idea, and when some people read this they will probably think that I am completely crazy. However, my experiences of the last few weeks tell me that in sharing my story, it does not matter what people think of me personally, as in this earthly existence there is nothing more painful to endure than the death of your child, and nothing of greater value that could be taken.

I am writing as someone who is not well known, well read or in any way remarkably different to any one else, but someone who is simply wife to John, mother to Jonathan and Edward, with an interesting career, and who lives in a nice house in the beautiful countryside in Shropshire.

Within a few days of Jonathan's death I felt that the only thing I wanted to do was to type out and share what had happened to me not just over the past few weeks, but over the last few years. The story is of a journey of faith, and by its nature some parts are very personal. In fact, I have found it is far easier to write it all down than to talk about it. Although some of it might seem unbelievable, it is totally true. In committing this to paper I have no wish to persuade anyone that they must believe the same as I do. It is much simpler.

My purpose in writing is to raise awareness of the spiritual journey that is there for everyone. For some it may be something that you have never really thought about, others may recognise that they are on a path but maybe their exploration is on the back burner, while others will know that they have got a lot further than I have. Jonathan's death has been the prompt to me to set out my thoughts, and my greatest wish is that in reading them you will resolve to start, or continue your spiritual journey. It doesn't matter what you know, who you are, where you are at in life or whether you subscribe to a religion. I am not a teacher, I certainly haven't got the answers, but I would like to be the catalyst that encourages you to explore for yourself, and come to your own conclusions. I hope that wherever you are on your spiritual journey, my words will be the inspiration that you need. In sharing my thoughts I know that if each of you took some positive action on your spiritual path, the world would be a better place, and in that way losing Jonathan would have made a much needed contribution.

In writing this it doesn't matter to me whether this manuscript is read by just a few people or whether it is read by thousands. If it sets just one person on their journey of faith, or gives hope to someone with theirs, it will have been worthwhile. I have no idea where this will lead. When I started writing, I was not sure if it was an end or a beginning, but I knew then as I know now, that for whatever reason I was meant to write this, and that I am content to rely on my relationship with God for guidance.

About ten days after Jonathan's death John read some words of wisdom to me from the Dalai Lama, which couldn't have summed up better what I want to say. His advice was that it is no good planting a tree when you see a storm brewing on the horizon. The time to plant the tree is in calm times, so that when the storm comes it has grown some roots. Then it is able to withstand the battering and hold firm. I dug the hole and started planting my tree several years ago, and the roots that have grown have enabled me to hold on over the last three months. In many ways my roots have become stronger, and many people have commented on my strength. This is my story.

One – An Ordinary Life

I was born in 1954 into a loving family. I have a younger sister Pat and brother Paul whom, being ten years younger than I am, I still consider the baby of the family. We grew up in Kent, my Dad worked at a local factory, and Mum looked after us. My childhood was happy and we did what youngsters did in those days.

I was taken along to Sunday school, and remember being very pleased with myself for winning a prize in a national scripture exam. I went to the Church Youth Club and enjoyed having some fun. I was asked if I would like to be confirmed with some of my contemporaries but declined as, although I enjoyed the company, that was really all there was to it. I look back on this as a moral foundation rather than a spiritual one and remember specifically how boring I thought praying was.

In 1970 I met John and knew straight away that he was the one for me, although I think it is fair to say that he wasn't quite so sure that I was the one for him! The outcome of this was that in 1973 I took myself off to Southampton University to study Psychology and Statistics. No one in our family had been to University before, but I was sure I was just as capable as other people who had secured places, and I thought, why not me. John encouraged me to take my opportunity, and we agreed that if we did decide to spend our future together we would take it from there. The old saying, 'absence makes the heart grow fonder' proved to be true, and by the end of the year we were engaged and were married the following year, while I was still a student.

Although I had originally intended to follow my degree with a teacher training course, I got the chance to spend an extra year in Southampton studying Social Statistics and left in 1977 with an M.Sc. John and I both got good jobs in the Midlands and settled down to a life of buying houses, career building, going travelling, purchasing sports cars and generally having a jolly good time.

We were very happy, everything seemed to fall into place for me, and people commented on my good fortune. I realised many years later that this reflected my ability to see opportunities and actually act upon them, but even then I had a feeling that one day I would inevitably have to face some disaster. Maybe this was the statistician in me, reminding me of the laws of probability that if you live a full life there is going to be both pain and pleasure. This thought resurfaced periodically, and I can remember very specifically several conversations where I shared these concerns with people.

It took several years for John to be persuaded that we could be as happy, or even happier, if we ventured into parenthood, but a delightful son of one of our friends finally helped me tip the balance, and our beautiful son Jonathan was born in June 1983.

The arrival of a child brings many changes and as we both had careers there was some discussion about who would take the role of principal carer. I was employed as Research, Information and Development Officer for Dudley Social Services, and I initially returned to work and a nanny came to the house and looked after Jonathan. However, I knew I really wanted to be at home and having dabbled in selling children's clothes, I was attracted to the flexibility of being self-employed. By the time Jonathan was a year old, John had got a local government post in Shropshire and I had decided to set up my own small business. Neither we nor our families had any experience of running a small business and it was all quite exciting.

In September 1985 we had our younger son Edward, and watched our two little boys grow up together. Initially the business, which was called 'Togs for Tots', only required a small amount of time and it fitted in very well with the demands of two small children. The business became more successful than we ever anticipated and by the time Jonathan started school I was selling clothes, delivering nappies and hiring out baby equipment. We needed extra space and moved to Nesscliffe, living in a caravan for six months while the old farm buildings we had bought were turned into a spacious house. Eventually the business also included the shop at our local maternity unit.

We had a lot of fun and satisfaction building Togs for Tots, but ultimately I decided that I had developed every avenue I could, and started looking for something else. Through a chance meeting on a plane returning from one of our many happy family holidays in Tenerife, I came across the opportunity to set up a network marketing business with a publishing company called Dorling Kindersley (DK) and decided to join. Although I had chosen not to follow a career in teaching, I had always been interested in education, and this seemed ideal. In running my own businesses, and bringing up two young boys, I had many experiences and often joked that I could write a book about them!

In 1996 I decided that I would attempt to keep Togs for Tots, which now included seven part time employees and a turnover in excess of £250,000, ticking over and build up the new DK business at the same time. Remaining enthusiastic about Togs for Tots while concentrating my efforts on an exciting new business was one of the biggest business challenges of my life. As the DK business became more successful so the pressure on me became greater.

Jonathan and Edward had moved on to the Oswestry School, and I kept myself very busy with both businesses. Added to that, after nearly thirty years in local government, John had decided to become self-employed, which meant that he was simply no longer around as much to give me the support that he had over the years. At the end of 1998 we finally agreed that things couldn't continue like this, and that Togs for Tots would have to go.

In the last thirty years, like many people, I had only briefly thought about the spiritual side to life when invited to christenings, weddings and funerals. Everything in life had gone well for me; I had everything anyone could want; a lovely husband, two super boys, a nice house, successful businesses, good friends and family, money to buy things. I knew the difference between right and wrong, had tried to be helpful and kind to my fellow citizens and considered I lived a decent life. I felt no need to look any further; after all what would I be looking for? Not only that, I really didn't have time as I was far too busy to add anything else to my hectic lifestyle.

In 1999 the sale of Togs for Tots started a sequence of events that made me think very differently.

Two – The Peace Which Passes All Understanding

'Busy' is a gross under-description of my life in February 1999. With everything else to do, I now had a buyer for Togs for Tots and had to deal with the sale of a business. I was working hard at my DK business, and there was a good chance of my meeting the criteria to win a trip to Barcelona. Although our buyer was keen to purchase Togs for Tots, there was a series of unexpected hitches and the sale progressed incredibly slowly.

In the middle of February I had also been admitted to the Royal Shrewsbury Hospital as an outpatient for a laparoscopy for a recurrent gynaecological problem. Although it was all straightforward, I did not respond well to the anaesthetic and was still being sick when I left in the evening. There was so much happening in every different aspect of my life.

Looking back it is obvious that as the pressures and demands on me had risen over a period of time, so had my stress levels. I didn't realise it, but I was virtually at breaking point. The one thing I do remember is that I started to say to myself and to John "I can't cope". John tried to reassure me that the pressure at present was temporary, and that it would be relieved by the sale of Togs for Tots. I had never thought like this before in my life. Others knew Julie as the well-organised person who always coped.

Physically I started to find everything hard work and I felt so tired that, although I felt terribly guilty, I started having a sleep in the afternoon. Every now and then I had the sensation of being dizzy, but within a few seconds I recovered. Paracetamol and other non-prescription drugs kept me going through the day, but by this stage nothing could avert the misery that was to come.

The final straw came one Friday morning in the middle of March. Jonathan and Edward had gone to school, John had gone to Tamworth, and I planned to go out to take the car for a repair. I also intended to do numerous other activities and be at a nursery for a lunchtime DK event. I did not feel 100% but that was nothing new. I had a few things to do in the office before I went. Sue was there sorting out paperwork for Togs for Tots. The phone rang with another piece of news I could have done without. As I sat at my desk, I started to feel so dizzy that I crossed my arms and put my head on them. I felt sick, my head was spinning, I couldn't move and I started hyperventilating. Sue rang 999.

I was still slouched across the desk when the ambulance arrived. The ambulance team tried to stabilise my breathing by getting me to breathe deeply, got me up, stood on either side of me and half carried me to the ambulance. Even lying down the dizziness was unbearable, totally incapacitating and frightening. My head continued to spin and I was afraid that I would lose consciousness. Blue flashing light and sirens blaring, we made the ten-minute trip to the Accident & Emergency Dept at the Royal Shrewsbury Hospital.

I lay on the trolley at the hospital feeling very unwell, and willing to accept anything that would get rid of the dizziness. I had had a dizzy episode caused by an ear infection many years before, and I remembered the doctor giving me an injection and I presumed that this is what I would be given at the hospital.

Meanwhile Sue had rung John and he had rushed to the hospital as quickly as he could from Tamworth. I lay in the A&E Department; terrified when I had the dizzy sensations and terrified when I didn't, in case they came back. We were there for the rest of the morning and into the afternoon, until the symptoms had subsided and we struggled home. I was told to make an appointment at the doctors, and that I probably had something called labyrinthitis, which is an inflammation of the part of the inner ear responsible for maintaining balance.

I tried to take things easy. The general consensus was that a holiday would do me good, and in fact we had booked to go to Tenerife in the first week of April. I was very concerned about the effect on my ears of the pressure in the plane, but I had some pills to control the dizziness, and I desperately wanted to get away on holiday.

We had a leisurely week in Tenerife, but as soon as we returned I knew I really needed more than a week to feel better. Everyone tried to help, and John took over some of the DK events for me, but every task was hard work. I kept feeling dizzy and was constantly afraid I would get really dizzy again and collapse in a heap.

In the meantime I had qualified for the DK trip to Barcelona, and I began to wonder whether or not to go. On the one hand I knew that I would be terribly disappointed if I did not go, but on the other I was concerned whether I would be well enough. As the trip drew nearer I decided to go to the doctor and seek his advice. He listened to my concerns and we agreed that I should go and see a consultant concerning the supposed labyrinthitis before I went abroad again. I took the option of a private consultation and got an appointment within a few days.

It was convenient to put the episode in the office down to the medical condition labyrinthitis; I could put on a brave face but I knew how dreadful I felt. I was so tired and I knew that physically I had pushed myself to the limit. I kept struggling along knowing that there was more to it than the clinical diagnosis I had been given. I began to think that somehow these were the symptoms of being stressed out, something about which I had read, but of which I had no real understanding. I distinctly remember tentatively asking the doctor if the symptoms of dizziness could be due to stress. He said that he thought not.

I saw the consultant a week before we were due to leave for the four-day trip to Barcelona. I was there for at least half an hour while he did all sorts of tests on my hearing and examined inside my ears. He told me he could find absolutely nothing wrong with me, and that I did not have labyrinthitis, with which he would have expected to find some loss of hearing. There was no medical reason not to fly to Barcelona. What he said was "I can't tell you whether you should go on your trip or not. You will have to choose between the anxiety that it will cause you to go, and the anxiety it will cause you if you don't go". I knew he was right - no truer words could have been spoken. My visit to the consultant had brought so much clarity, that I felt immediately better, and decided I would go to Barcelona.

Mum and Dad had arrived to look after Jonathan and Edward for us, and on Thursday 13th May we headed off on the long awaited trip. Even though I knew that John would look after me, I was anxious about whether I had made the right decision. The trip was a celebration of achievements, but I just wanted to be in a quiet place.

We arrived in Barcelona after lunch and I was looking forward to getting to the hotel and having a lie down. However the itinerary included a tour of Barcelona first, which I would rather have avoided. It was a relief when we eventually got there, and we prepared to go out for the evening meal. I could hardly eat anything and found it very difficult to socialise. I was glad to get out of the restaurant for five minutes and phone home.

The next day we were taken out for a morning trip around the park created by Gaudi. The coach dropped us off and we made our own way back to the hotel, stopping for a late lunch on the way. It was all very pleasant but I felt anxious and weak. I can't remember anything more except waking up in a state of panic on the Saturday morning, saying to John 'I can't stay here I want to go home'. John went and spoke to the organisers of the trip, who did everything possible and booked a flight back to the UK for us that afternoon. We said goodbye to our DK friends amid the tears, and left for the airport. How I got home I do not know.

We had returned, and I was exhausted. On the Sunday morning everyone rallied round and made dinner and I stayed in bed. This was to be the place I was most likely to be found over the next few weeks.

Everyone worked around me, Sue came in to the office and kept Togs for Tots running, the boys came and said goodbye to me in bed before they got the school bus, and John would bring me a drink and some fruit, which was all I could manage in the morning, before he went to work. I tried to get up sometime in the afternoon, and build up enough courage and resources to go out and do simple everyday tasks like shopping for food.

I went to the doctors and without hesitation he prescribed Seroxat, a course of anti-depressants, which to start with made me feel even worse. I persevered.

I spent three months barely holding myself together. I was tired, I had lost weight, I was afraid, I felt sick, I had headaches, I felt panicky, and not surprisingly I was depressed. This was the lowest point in my life. I felt I was in the bottom of a black hole and I didn't know the way out. I had spent months gaining first-hand experience of the meaning of the words depression and stress, and it was dreadful. I felt so bad, and knew that mentally I had visited places that I never, ever wanted to visit again.

I did not know if I would ever recover my enthusiasm for life, but John never lost faith that I would find my old self, and he and others gave me words, cards and little presents of hope which I treasured. The sale of Togs for Tots was finally progressing, and this in itself would remove a lot of pressure. I knew that simply the passage of time would make things seem better.

Having spent hours in bed I had had plenty of time to think about how I had lived my life, and where it had led me. I started to think that there must be more to life than this. If ever I needed God this was the time, and although I didn't really know where to start I began to pray the only prayer I knew, which was The Lord's Prayer and to ask for guidance out of this mess.

I continued praying every night when I went to bed, hoping that this would help my situation. I wanted to wake up the next day feeling my old enthusiastic positive self. I wanted a miracle to happen and in a way it did.

Prayers, to me, had always been a bunch of words that people recited. I thought you said prayers in the hope that they would help with the business of living, and as a kind of insurance for the long term. As the nights went on, I started to pray dwelling more on the words and the meaning. I felt more inclined to cling less to my outer protective shell and to open up to God in my prayers. Eventually I acknowledged that for all my worldly successes, I had not arrived at a place I wanted to be. I felt so desperate, and there seemed to be some comfort in prayer.

Finally, one night, my prayers took me a step further. I asked God to be a part of my life in a way that I had never done before. With total conviction, I offered my life back to God and promised to listen for guidance in future. My surrender came from somewhere within, and although I had no idea how I might go forward, my whole body felt flooded with such peace that I knew I would never go back on my commitment. All I could think of was a phrase that I had heard; I had no idea where it was from, but that I had experienced 'the peace which passes all understanding'.

My prayers were answered that night in a way that I did not anticipate and could never have imagined, but the power of that response has remained with me ever since. From that moment I was absolutely certain that God would show me what to do with my life.

The next day I wanted to tell people about this experience, but whom could I tell? I had never spoken much about anything spiritual to John, my family or my friends and I felt that people would think I had lost my senses. It was such a personal experience, and I didn't know how to start to share it, so I just decided that all I could do was accept that it was something that would be followed up in some way. It was over a year later before I told anyone about my experience that night.

I believe that my slow recovery was aided by time, and by outside influence - support from friends, by the pills from the doctor, by this spiritual turning point, but also with the realisation that I could help myself.

Through the DK business, both John and I had got interested again in personal development and had collected a few books and some meditation tapes. My efforts at meditating were hopeless. No matter how I tried, I simply could not sit still and clear my mind for a few minutes let alone twenty minutes. I gave up, and it was not until quite a while later that I realised that there is a dual meaning when people talk about practising meditation. On the surface it seems as though it should be such an easy thing to do, but this is not necessarily the case, and results come literally from practising.

Again my knowledge of personal development made me aware that from the time I had started saying to myself and John that I could not cope, I was not sending a very useful message to my subconscious. I remember standing in the shower and thinking up an affirmation to expect a great day. I did not believe it, but I knew that did not necessarily matter. I told myself repeatedly in the morning and through the day "I can cope, and that it will be a wonderful day". I did this for several weeks and I felt much better.

As the sale of Togs for Tots became imminent I thought about all that I had learned about running my first small business. Many challenges had been tackled and overcome in the last fifteen years, but it wasn't the business challenges that had been the tricky ones, it was the personal ones that overlapped with it. More than anything I realised the foolishness of harbouring a sense of bitterness or anger against anything or anyone that had upset or annoyed me. I knew that for many years I had let a deteriorating relationship eat away at me. At the time it seemed the easy option to let the situation continue. However, looking back I could see how I had allowed my energy to be drained, and realised I should have faced it and dealt with it.

I learned much from my experience of being stressed out. The impact that my way of thinking had on my physical wellbeing was inescapable. After ignoring the warning signs that my body was sending out, it eventually gave up and shut down all but the essential systems. This is what happens - it is the body's natural defence system. I had already been taking steps to reduce the pressure, but I didn't get the timing right. I resolved to go forward in a different way with a new lifestyle that paid attention to, and took time for, mind, body and spirit.

The sale of Togs for Tots finally went through at the beginning of July, and I slowly started to pick up the pieces of my life. In September 1999 John and I celebrated our 25th wedding anniversary, and although I was still a bit apprehensive, I enjoyed the party we had for family and friends at the village hall a few weeks later. I gradually reduced my reliance on Seroxat and looked forward to the New Year.

Three – Simply Beyond Coincidence

We celebrated the new millennium at a friend's house and I looked forward to a much better year. A huge weight had been lifted in the sale of Togs for Tots, and at last I could concentrate on building my DK business. Things went well. Although I was successful, I was never that keen on the retailing side; the part I really loved was building relationships with the team members, and helping them toward the level of success that they had determined. After the abortive trip to Barcelona, I really wanted to qualify for the next DK trip, which was to Cyprus, and several team members committed to doing this as well. By March three of us had achieved this goal, and in doing this together I realised that by far the greatest joy came from helping others in my team to achieve their dreams. There was a level of satisfaction well above that of personal success.

I never forgot my commitment to God and I prayed most nights. As an individual I still felt a bit fragile. I felt as though I was still recovering from the trauma of the previous year, but I also thought I was at the right place and that one day something would somehow happen.

My interest in the personal development books continued with my reading the occasional book, thinking it would help me to build my business. We had been receiving a catalogue from a company that produced audio cassettes, which John was more into than me as he liked listening to them in the car, when one day in April their latest brochure dropped through the letter box. Out of it fell a flyer about a motivational speaker from the US who would be in London in July. We both thought it looked interesting, and John faxed back to get more details.

The information that we had requested arrived, and it sounded absolutely fascinating. The weekend seminar promised to find out what you want from life, how to inspire yourself and others, and how to create unstoppable momentum in the achievement and fulfilment of your life. I thought maybe this was the new start I was looking for. There was one slight problem, the course itself cost nearly £800, and then there were all the expenses of getting to

London and staying overnight. For that kind of money, all four of us could go on a holiday!

The information booklet stayed on the kitchen table and John and I never discussed it, as I think we had both looked at the cost and that was that, there really was nothing to talk about. I felt drawn to this booklet and kept looking at it and thinking that going to something like this would be quite an experience. In my head I discussed it with myself - maybe I should tell John I would like to go, but then maybe not. In the end I never said anything to John, and resigned myself to the fact that there was no way I could justify the expense of going to this. I decided that the best way for me to find out what this American guru had to say was to go and buy his book. It was a Friday morning, I was going into town, and decided to go into Waterstones and have a look– there was one copy of *Awaken the Giant Within (1)* by Anthony Robbins, which I bought.

I had agreed to deliver some DK books later that morning, and had a little time to pass, so I went round the corner to a coffee shop and got out my new purchase and started reading the first few pages. I always carried my mobile phone, which the boys jokingly referred to as a 'brick', for emergency use but in those days I never had it turned on, and not surprisingly I never received any phone calls. For some reason that day while in the coffee shop, I thought to reach into my bag and switch the mobile on. I was quite engrossed reading, and could see that this was a book I would enjoy. Maybe I should say something to John about going to this weekend event after all.

I got in the car and drove the short drive to do my delivery and just as I pulled up, to my absolute amazement, my mobile phone started ringing. It was John. I was completely dumbstruck when he said, "I have had a phone call from the Tony Robbins organisation." He continued that there were some 'buy one, get one free' tickets on offer for the weekend in London. Although John had got something on, and could not go, the salesman said that if I wanted to go, he would let me have the ticket at half price and he would sell the other one. Knowing everything I had thought and done that morning, I could not believe that John, knowing none of this, was ringing me and saying effectively if you want to go, then go. The idea of going to London on my own to an event about which I knew very little was scary, but I could not ignore the thoughts that I had had, or the unbelievable combination of events that had come together. What happened that morning to me was simply beyond coincidence, and I was certain that I was meant to be there.

John said he would ring the salesman back, and say I was interested in the half price ticket, and ask him to ring me at home at 2pm to confirm the details. He rang and I booked the weekend. Just a few hours before, I could see no way that I would be in London in July, and to this day I find the sequence of events quite incredible. At that stage, I knew I had to be there, but didn't really know why; in fact it was impossible to even conceive of the ways that the weekend would alter the course of my life.

Initially I was so excited that I was going to the Tony Robbins event in London, called 'Unleash the Power Within'. However, it was one of those things that having said yes, I began to think, what I have done? Would I come back brainwashed? Even would I come back? When I started to think about it, I really did not know what I was going to, apart from what I had read in the brochure and what the salesman had told me. I started to worry about the length of the sessions, and whether I would be able to keep awake, as the schedule started early and went on late. I didn't particularly want to stay in a hotel for three nights on my own, and so I rang Dad's brother Frank and his wife Irene, who live near Wembley, to see if there was any chance of staying with them for the weekend. They kindly agreed to provide my accommodation and things were left at that.

May 17th arrived and we met up with DK friends for the eagerly awaited trip to Cyprus. We had a wonderful time. I tentatively mentioned to a few people that I had booked to see this American motivational speaker, and was sure it would help me, and my DK business, but got equally tentative responses. No one had seen him, but they had heard about him! Help! After the words of wisdom I received, I thought maybe cancelling would be the best option. The only encouraging comment was that there might be some value if it is at the right time in your life. This left me feeling totally discouraged from even mentioning it to anyone else.

I left home at the end of June for the drive to Frank and Irene's, saying to John not to be surprised if I returned the following day. I did not necessarily want to make great changes in my life. I had learned a lot through my illness the previous year and was reasonably happy. I had never heard a motivational speaker with celebrity status before, but I was sure that I could learn from him and apply it on both a business and a personal level. I tried to justify to myself the reasons for my wanting to be there – I did want to make some changes to my attitude to diet and exercise as I knew this would improve my physical health, and I hoped it would make me feel a bit more energetic.

When I got to Irene's she offered to show me the route from her house to the Wembley Arena. I was quite excited on one hand but also terribly nervous, not only about the event but also the practical side of driving back from this event at 2am, and then getting up a few hours later to be there again for 10am. When we got to the Wembley Arena there were long queues of people waiting to get in. There seemed no point rushing to join the queue, so we went back to the house for a cup of tea.

Four – A Life Changing Weekend

By the time I got back to the Wembley Arena there were no queues. There was music and the event was just starting. I rushed up the stairs and sat myself down where there weren't too many people around. Along with the crowd of 3000 people I listened as Tony Robbins introduced the weekend. I was spellbound by his presence, and felt an instant connection with what he was saying. I knew then I would not be going home on Saturday.

It was a fascinating evening about overcoming fears and culminating in the most publicised part of Tony Robbins events, a fire walk. I felt rather pleased that I had walked across the burning coals, but it was now 2am and I hoped that I would have some energy for the next day. I managed to find the way back to Frank and Irene's and to bed. As I lay in bed thinking about the evening, the soles of my feet felt like they were glowing. Afterwards I thought it might have been sensible to wash them!

There were many practical exercises over an unforgettable weekend full of experiences, and many highlights far too many to mention here, but I can vividly remember two particular insights.

One exercise required one of us to think of a particular emotional situation that we had experienced, and recall it matching our physical positions, breathing etc. Another person was asked to copy these physical characteristics assisted by a helper. This person then tried to feel the emotions of the other person through maintaining their physical position and, if they could, to describe the actual situation. We all took turns and we were all able to identify the other person's emotions, and I surprised myself at how close I was to describing what was actually happening. I felt my partner was a nervous flyer and was on a plane taxiing along the runway - in fact he was on a plane but he was about to make his first parachute jump! I was amazed that some of the people in the audience had been able to witness the emotions and events that the other person was experiencing with absolute accuracy. This was a wonderful experience and a demonstration of the ability we all have to communicate on a non-verbal level.

The most moving experience for me was when we were asked to find a number of different people and look into their eyes with love and to continue transferring increasing love. By this stage of the weekend many of the barriers that would normally inhibit people had gone, and everyone was participating even in what seemed the strangest requests. I could feel a sense of love in everyone's eyes, but the eyes of the very last person simply met my soul. He whispered a few words to me, which indicated that he too was deeply moved by this experience. We went back to our seats and I never saw him again, I didn't need to. A sense of love had been transferred between two complete strangers. What purer level of communication could there be between people?

There were so many people and as I knew no one, I chatted with anyone I happened to be with, which included a variety of people. One chap observed how important my family was to me and told me that he would like to be married. He thought the answer was to increase his bank balance so that he became more eligible. I hope he learned something from the weekend.

Despite what I had been told, Tony Robbins seemed to me to be a totally sincere person, doing what he was good at. I was interested in the way he acknowledged the role of God in our lives, and made it quite clear that he held Christian beliefs.

As might be expected, there was a certain amount of raising interest in, and marketing the next Tony Robbins event, which sounded great. However, the one thing that I noted was that there were opportunities to follow up this event working with a professional coach who would help you to follow through with your commitments to change. I thought this was a great idea, having been on plenty of training courses where the intention to follow up was inevitably good but often nothing happened, because there was no follow up support. What was most interesting to me was that the Tony Robbins organisation was looking for people to train as coaches, to work with those who had been at the event. The DK business had shown me the pleasure that was to be had from helping others to overcome challenges and achieve their goals, and I wrote down all the details. I was familiar with the idea of a sports coach, but had never heard the word coach in this context before, and had no idea that there was a whole new profession called life coaching emerging in the UK.

The intensity of the course, which was invigorating rather than tiring, meant that I hardly saw Frank and Irene. However, I do remember telling them that I was most interested in this idea of coaching, had written down all the details, and thought I would follow it up. I had no idea how.

I had made many changes in lifestyle since being so ill, and on a personal level I had attended the weekend with health and fitness in mind. My experiences had left me in no doubt that physical well-being and mental well-being are inextricably linked, and many of the healthy living ideas were not new to me. John and I were already working toward some of them, so I took up what was referred to as the 'ten day challenge', knowing that there were some new ideas as well as some familiar ones. The challenge was to see if changes of lifestyle made you feel any different, and if so to extend it to thirty days and thereby establish new habits.

The 'ten day challenge' consisted of deep breathing exercises every day, increasing water intake, aerobic exercise three times a week, only fruit and juices in the morning, 'food combining' avoiding starch and protein in the same meal, a directed positive mindset, taking care of the physical structure of the body and eliminating excess fats, animal flesh, dairy products, sugar, salt, alcohol and caffeine from the diet where possible. I also decided not to take any more Paracetamol or non-prescription drugs unless I was really able to justify them, so that I knew exactly how the physical 'me' felt. I did what I could of this lengthy list immediately and gradually built in the other changes. I did feel better for my change of lifestyle; after all it was only really about respecting and taking care of my physical self. An added benefit was that I returned to my pre-Jonathan weight. Three years later this different way of living is part of life for both John and me, and some of our friends think we are mad!

After four long days at the event I drove home feeling energised, excited and confident. I was so pleased that I had mustered the courage to go, and had so much to tell John. I was talking about it for weeks after, so much so that John said he thought he had better go along next time.

Back to the reality of general life, the laparoscopy operation the previous year had not revealed the cause of the mid monthly pain I suffered. Sometimes it was so bad that I could hardly stand up, and painkillers did very little. When I struggled home from our shop some years before, I had said to John to remind me of that evening if I even started to hesitate about having an operation. Since the laparoscopy I had had various drug treatments, which got rid of the pain but were unsuitable for long-term use. Two days after my return from London I had an appointment with a consultant.

The consultant was very nice, and explained that the tests showed that there really was no other option to get rid of the pain except a full hysterectomy: womb, ovaries and fallopian tubes. He did not actually know what the cause of the pain was, but the drugs had shown that taking everything out was the only way he could guarantee the required result. He suggested that I have the operation as soon as possible. He explained that it was a major operation and that I would not be able to do anything for six weeks, plus there would be a longer full recovery period. I asked him what the downsides might be after recovery, and he proceeded to reel off various statistics of the likelihood of possible after effects. The only one that I can remember was loss of sex drive, which was extremely high, and I remember thinking that the percentage he was quoting only represented those who report it!

If the consultant had said this is what he had found, this is the cause, and this is the action we need to take, that would have been fine, but being advised to have a major operation without an identifiable cause seemed crazy to me. Three days before I had listened to Tony Robbins illustrating the plight of doctors, who, under pressure of work, can often only stand by the river bank watching their patients being drawn along by the current and pluck them out to save them from drowning, but never have the time to go along the river bank and find the cause of them falling in in the first place. I felt that the consultant was simply offering to pluck me out of the river.

I thought about the mind/body connection, and the previous year when my whole physical being had been shut down by the effect of stress. I had just committed myself to a new lifestyle and I thought maybe this is what I needed, rather than an operation. I thanked him for his time and told him that at the present time I did not want to take up his offer, but that I was going to try changing my lifestyle first. He said to remember that he could offer me at least five years freedom from pain, but I knew his offer would be available another day. I walked out of the consulting room pleased that I had the confidence to say No, but also wondering whether the investigations might have missed something that needed an operation. I went home to put my healthy lifestyle into place, and although the pains have never completely gone, I no longer take painkillers and have never looked back. How fortunate it was that the appointment had followed my weekend adventure – the price of the ticket was more than repaid to me in the way I had been able to respond that morning.

Five - An Unexpected Path Appears

Oswestry School was due to break up for summer, and we had arranged to leave for a week away in Wales immediately after Speech Day. Apart from Jonathan falling off his skateboard and hurting himself about five minutes after we arrived, it was an enjoyable week together. I was looking forward to returning to my new lifestyle and continuing to build my DK business. My team was rapidly expanding and I fully expected to reach Director Level within the next two years.

We returned from holiday in the middle of July, and on the following day received a phone call from our upline DK Director, Russell. He was ringing to say that he and everyone at Director Level had been called to an important meeting the coming week and he was not expecting the announcement to be good. Earlier that year DK had been bought out by Pearsons, and although there had been some uncertainty, we were assured that with their resources this would secure a better future. He said he would be in touch.

A few days later, before I got the promised phone call, a colleague rang and told me that she had heard that the whole of the direct sales division of DK, of which I and 60,000 people worldwide were part, was to be closed down pretty well immediately. Russell rang with confirmation, and told me what had happened in the meeting, how buyout attempts had been put forward and rejected, and said that in fact letters terminating our contracts had already been posted. We were all gutted.

The next day the letters arrived on doorsteps, basically advising us that Pearsons had made a business decision based on the viability of the direct sales business worldwide, and giving us details of the closedown procedures to be followed. We had until the middle of August to place our final orders and take steps to wind up our independent businesses.

The phone started ringing with disbelieving and tearful team members. How could the company be allowed to do this? Many of us had spent years building our businesses, but the self-employed nature of our contracts meant we had no rights. No matter how many years we had spent with DK, or our level of income, we were all given the same short period of notice. It seemed grossly unfair. If any other type of company had made this number of employees redundant there would have been a national outcry.

I watched with interest at how people responded. There were those that wanted to make Pearsons pay for this suffering, and a fund was set up to fight for proper compensation. I never got involved because common sense told me that, although we might be able to make a few waves, our contracts were written to protect the company. Also, I did not want to be drawn into generating even more anger and bitterness than there already was. The energy-draining effect of these emotions had been a fundamental lesson that I had learned from my experience with Togs for Tots, and I did not need to repeat it.

I watched as some of my colleagues tried to railroad their teams into new network marketing businesses as a way of protecting their own income. Some of the people whom I had previously admired showed their true colours. Despite what they had previously led people to believe, in their desperation it was quite clear that helping themselves was far more important than helping their team.

I watched as people from other network marketing businesses jumped on the bandwagon and tried to recruit successful people from within DK. It was all very sad.

So it was that I, along with many others, found myself in the middle of a situation over which I had no control, and could do nothing to change. Having worked hard for four years, built a team of 240 people and with a reasonable and rapidly increasing income, I was left to ponder how someone else's decisions took it all away. I had done everything I could to make DK successful. I had chosen to sell Togs for Tots to concentrate on the DK business, and in doing so had gone from having two successful businesses the previous year, to be left with no business and no income. Looking back, I realised the significance of John's decision to become self-employed, and his ability to make a success of it. It had been instrumental in the sale of Togs for Tots, and now had turned into a financial lifesaver.

Over the last year I felt I had come a long way mentally, physically and spiritually. My mindset was very much that I could cope, and I started to see this situation as an opportunity for me and my team to think individually about what we wanted to do. My physical health was not brilliant, but there was no comparison with where I was last year, and I was actively working on it. Spiritually I had continued to pray for direction, and although I didn't know how things might turn out, I had no fear about the future. I felt that in all these events God was with me.

I have always approached things very logically, and was able to apply this approach quite easily when thinking about how to go forward. I knew what experience I had, what I was good at, and what I liked. I came up with five options. I had always felt drawn to teaching and thought about doing the teacher training course that I never did twenty five years before. I had loved building my businesses and felt there were many people that I could help and encourage, who may otherwise never have the confidence to try, so thought maybe I could be a small business advisor and decided to make some enquiries. I had done a little bit of training with DK and wondered if I could be a freelance trainer and arranged a couple of meetings with people that were doing this. My DK upline, Russell, was keen to keep me on board and he was putting together a business opportunity, which, although top secret, sounded promising. Also of course, just a few weeks before, I had been intrigued by the idea of training as a life coach with the Tony Robbins organisation.

I thought about teaching - my final thought, which is a sad reflection on teaching, was did I really want the lifestyle of a teacher? I had an interview with someone who worked as a small business advisor within a government organisation, and left wondering whether the bureaucracy would stifle every ounce of my enthusiasm, as it obviously had with his. I met up with a successful freelance trainer, but I didn't feel I had the right background. I looked on the Tony Robbins website and realised that to train as a coach with them you had to be multi lingual and have been on all their courses. I searched on the Internet under 'life coaching' for any other coach trainers and came up with an American organisation, but I didn't feel very comfortable with the virtual learning set up via the computer. I wanted to be able to talk to people. There was still the opportunity with Russell, with whom I had worked very successfully, so I decided that the best thing to do was to wait and see what he had come up with.

It was the end of July and my sister Pat, husband Mark and the family had planned to come to stay for the weekend. There was some kind of question mark over this visit, I am not sure why that was, but I do remember Pat saying there was something telling her that they should come, and they did. On the Sunday afternoon we decided that we would all head off for Telford Town Park, as there is plenty there to keep the children amused. I can clearly remember John and me sitting in the car waiting for them all to return. On the back seat there was a newspaper that Mark had brought, which John turned round and picked up to skim through while passing the time. As he looked at the back page, he said to me "look at this!" - there was a picture of someone fire walking, an article about Tony Robbins, about life coaching and the name of a UK based coach-training organisation. I was so excited; this was just what I had been looking for. I could hardly believe it. This was Mark's newspaper, not ours, and there was no way that we would have looked at that newspaper had my sister and her family not come to stay. I asked Mark if I could cut the article out, and have kept it safe ever since.

I wasted no time in getting in touch with what was then the British Coaching Academy. I spoke to a charming man and told him what had happened, and how I had been thinking through my options. His enthusiastic response to me was "You sound like a life coach!"

I had promised myself that I would not make a decision on how to go forward until I had seen what Russell was proposing. I agreed to encourage all the key members of my team to a meeting at our house to hear the plans. Although I knew very little about being a life coach, I felt everything pointed to me taking this path; the sequence of events that took me to London where I came across the idea, the sudden and unexpected opportunity to follow it up because of the imminent closure of the DK business, and the more than fortuitous visit by my sister that led me to an article in a newspaper! Whatever the new business proposal was, I knew that it would have to be pretty impressive for me to follow.

I am sure that everyone attending the new business opportunity meeting that night would have his or her own recollection of the anticipation of this presentation. I sat there feeling distinctly uncomfortable. I knew that my response as a team leader would have an effect in determining how other people responded, and it was important that I made my position clear first, because my decision would determine the basis of how the team structure of the new organisation would be set up.

As a new range of kitchenware was unveiled, along with an exciting business opportunity, I couldn't have been more certain that this was not for me. At the end of the presentation, it was suggested that we discussed what we had seen over a cup of tea. I took my chance to have a quiet word with the presenter, and she was visibly stunned when I told her that I would not be joining the new organisation.

We went back into the meeting room and I told my team that I had wanted to check out all my options, and having now done that, I would not be joining them, but that I had decided to train to be a life coach. The room went absolutely silent. It was acknowledged that my choice was not the easy option. I had a ready-made sales team, many of whom would have followed me in to the new business. Some of the team signed up to the new company there and then, others were not sure and went home to think about it, and I was wished every success with my new venture. I was sorry that I had broken the business ties with my friends, but the real friends understood. I had to do what was right, and I wanted to continue to support them in doing the same.

The next month or so was spent bringing to a close a business that I loved, and I booked on the life coaching course for the end of October.

It was school summer holidays and we had arranged to spend a week in Kent and go to the Millennium Dome with Pat, Mark and family to celebrate their 20th Wedding Anniversary. Jonathan and Edward went off with them to explore the more exciting exhibits while John and I visited the relaxation and the religion section. I think we were both moved by some of what we read, and I particularly remember thinking very carefully about recent events, before contributing to a section which invited the participant to offer their message to the world. On my slip of paper I wrote 'the more you give, the more you get'. I believe the intention is to open these in 2050, but maybe they are thoughts that the world needs now.

Six – Life Journey and Spiritual Journey Meet

It was just over a year since I had dug myself out of my self made pit with the help of medicine, a positive attitude and God, and it would have been quite easy with events as they were to have fallen back into it. However, the feelings of depression and desperation did not re-emerge. I had learned a lot and I wanted to learn more.

Following my commitment to the 'ten day challenge' and regular aerobic exercise, I knew that I must do something that didn't take too much time out of the day, and that I could enjoy. It would be true to say that with any kind of athletic exercise, like many other people, I like watching rather than doing, and I find it difficult to muster much enthusiasm. Several years previously I had tried going to the gym, and decided that it was not for me. Very half heartedly, I decided the easiest thing to meet the commitment was a combination of walking and jogging, and made it a bit more interesting by buying a heart rate monitor. At least then I could check that I was doing what I was meant to do.

My enthusiasm for this activity gradually rose, not because I particularly liked the jogging, but more that going along the country lanes I could see such beauty in the flowers and the birds and the countryside. I had such a sense of freedom and of being close to nature, and to God. I would often come back and pull up a few weeds, feed the birds and just look round the garden. I thought about the saying 'don't forget to smell the roses' which I had first heard in DK, and really understood what it meant. Being able to take in nature is wonderful; it reawakens the senses.

I still had not told anyone about the spiritual experience I had had in response to my prayers the previous year, and wondered how I could follow it up. I was still thinking about this, when driving into Shrewsbury one day I saw an advertising hoarding, questioning the meaning of life. A very interesting question and a subject on which, many years ago, John and I had had an entertaining and memorable conversation with some good friends, which lasted well into the night. Needless to say we never came up with an answer. Within a few days of seeing the advert I saw something in the local newspaper raising the same question and offering a free course with a local contact. I went to the nearby Post Office, and as I stood looking at the advert board, this same information jumped out at me. After everything that had happened I knew better than to ignore the message that was being given to me, and I memorised the phone number and walked home.

I rang the number, and got through to a well-spoken gentleman called Adrian, who gave me the details. He said that although the introductory evening to the Alpha course had been the previous week, he would be delighted if we joined the group on the following Friday and I told him that I would be there. I told John what I had found out, and that I had said that I was definitely going along. I was really pleased when John said he would come too.

It was the 22nd September when we made our appearance at the tiny country village hall at Little Ness, not knowing what to expect. The format was that we all sat down to dinner, which Adrian's wife Brenda had prepared, allowing everyone an opportunity to meet the other members of the group. This was followed by a short video, and then we talked about the content. One thing I particularly remember was going round the group and everyone saying what they were there for. I gave a very limited answer, and said something about learning more, which was true, but I knew really I was hoping for a lot more than that.

Over the years I had noticed how many authors of personal development books mention a spiritual dimension to life, but then don't really go on to develop what they mean. I knew I didn't really understand. I had had a spiritual experience myself, which I could not explain, and wondered if the Alpha course could. Since that experience I had felt guided through events, which seemed to me to be beyond coincidence and toward what I hoped would be a new career in life coaching.

Several things struck me about the Alpha course. The first thing was the diversity of people; different ages, different backgrounds, different lifestyles and not really anyone there who I thought were like John and me. The second thing was the course itself. The initial topic was entitled Christianity – Boring, Untrue and Irrelevant? – which raised questions for us to think about and discuss, rather than being told what we ought to think. Although information was presented, the style of the course had very much a coaching feel to it, which I liked.

We enjoyed going along to the sessions; Brenda's dinners were great, the people were friendly, and although sometimes the discussion seemed to go in odd directions, it gave John and me something to think and talk about. I wanted to tell John about the real understanding for which I was looking, and as we started to talk more, it seemed that it would become easier. About three weeks into the course we were having our usual conversation about the topic of the evening as we drove home. When we pulled up outside the house I said to him that I wanted to tell him about something that had happened to me the previous year, which I had never shared with anyone. Looking back, I realise from John's response that he had no idea of the importance of what to me was a life-changing event. I don't know what I expected he would say, and neither of us can remember his exact response. However, my recollection is of a very short conversation ending with something along the lines of good for you, now let's go in and get a cup of tea! On reflection, I thought maybe it had been a mistake to say anything.

As the course unfolded I learned a lot, and some of the things I had experienced fell into place. I bought the book *Questions of Life (2)* that accompanied the course and found it useful to read while attending the sessions. I loved the way the course was illustrated with real life stories, anecdotes and even jokes; it met me at my simple level. Early on in the course we were told about a painting by William Holman Hunt called 'The Light of the World', which shows Jesus standing knocking at a door which symbolises a life. He wants to come in, but the door is apparently missing a handle, as there is only one on the inside. The whole point that the artist is making is that Jesus will knock, but he can't let himself in. It is entirely up to us as to whether we choose to open the door. It provides a powerful image, and I knew that a year ago I had opened that door.

My life seemed to be opening up in all directions, and just a few weeks after starting the Alpha course I headed off to Oxford to start the Life Coaching course. The course started with a residential weekend and I left Shropshire at the crack of dawn to get to Oxford for a 9.30am start on the Saturday morning. I didn't know anyone and again I didn't know what to expect. I just about arrived in time for the start and I went and sat at the front. I wish I hadn't because the first presenter was very animated and loud, and frightened the life out of me.

There were at least twenty people on the course and the idea was to be interactive. I did not feel particularly confident about contributing, and as people spoke I became less confident as I discovered I was surrounded by 'experts' in counselling, psychiatry, neurolinguistic programming, as well as various trainers and therapists. Although I knew a bit about all these things, I had never had any formal training in any of these disciplines, and felt completely out of my depth. I had walked away from the kind of self made business world I knew, John had decided to part with a substantial amount of his well earned income on this course, and I was beginning to think I had made a very big mistake. Although I enjoyed the actual content of the first day, particularly the listening module, I couldn't see how in this company I could make it as a professional coach, and it even crossed my mind to leave on Saturday night.

Saturday had been long and tiring, and when I arrived on the Sunday morning I hoped that things would get better. Eventually, on Sunday afternoon a speaker was introduced with whose background and style I could identify. I was so relieved that when she had finished I went and introduced myself, and thanked her for her presentation. I was so pleased I had met this lady; I didn't suppose that she would remember me, but I knew I would remember her. The course finished with a session on how to get a coaching practice up and running as a business - a subject that many of my course mates found a big challenge, but now my background was an asset. After all, what could possibly be the sense in having all this wonderful knowledge if you were unable to make use of it?

I left the weekend on a high, armed with my manual, ready to work through all the modules, the practice coaching calls, and all the other course requirements with a view to being an accredited life coach in six months. I decided to get my coaching practice set up as quickly as possible, and took the advice that was given at the end of the course which was to walk away from the training and practise saying, "I am a professional Life Coach".

I started promoting myself as a life coach simply by telling people what I was doing, and produced a short brochure that I could distribute. By the end of November, with the help of my good friend Julie, I had found my first paying client, and felt that my new career was really underway.

I settled down to building my coaching practice, completing the course modules and doing some background reading. I bought the recommended course books, and made a start. One of the first books I read was *Co-Active Coaching* (3), which in the front cover has a dedication to clients and coaches whose lives have been touched through coaching. Underneath is the story I had never heard before, which, as it says, illustrates the essence of co-active coaching and what it means to be a life coach. I was so moved by this story; it seemed to resonate with the very essence of me.

The story goes that early one morning a man was walking along the beach, watching the waves breaking on the shore, and he saw a most unusual thing. He saw that the beach was littered with thousands of starfish that had been washed up on shore and were dying in the sun. Far down the beach in the distance, he could see a young woman picking up starfish and throwing them back into the ocean, one at a time. When he was close enough to her to be heard above the waves, the man said, "You're wasting your time. There are thousands of starfish here. You can't possibly make any difference." The young woman reached down, picked up a starfish and threw it as far as she could back into the sea. "I made a difference to that one", she said and reached down to pick up another. This story had a profound impact on me, but I had no idea that the real significance was about to be revealed.

John and I were still attending the Alpha course, which raised all sorts of questions. No one claimed to have all the answers, which was just as well, as the last thing we wanted was to be told what to believe. I was amazed at how such a mixed bunch of people seemed to hit it off. As we got to know each other I felt drawn to a lady called Anne. In age, background and experience she was very different to me, but it was quite clear that we had some very similar thoughts. I distinctly remember us having a little discussion about the difficulties that could be raised if a couple in a relationship had no understanding of the spiritual needs of their partner. We were both glad that we had both attended the Alpha course together with our husbands.

As Christmas approached the Alpha course was coming to its conclusion. There were several occasions when I nearly told of my experience the previous year, and how since then so many things had come in to my life and shaped my direction in a way that no one could have ever imagined. It seemed to me that when you start asking for guidance from God, get a response, and then so many what seem to be unrelated coincidences all point in the same direction, you are left with no other conclusion except that this is how it is meant to be.

I knew I had a wonderful story, but the moment to share it seemed to keep passing by. Due to the limited number of weeks up to Christmas, Adrian had missed one or two videos which meant that when we got to the last week, the one we watched was out of sequence, and should have been viewed several weeks earlier. As usual we enjoyed our dinner together, got the video going and sat back. I felt completely overwhelmed when the story which effectively brought these sessions to a conclusion was: "There was a man walking along the beach, watching the waves breaking on the shore, and he saw a most unusual thing ……".That evening my life journey and my spiritual journey met.

When the film finished, I briefly told my story to the group. I was so overcome with emotion I struggled to speak, but I wanted to tell them. It was really what I had wanted to do all along.

Seven – Listening

One of the ideas I had picked up through my coaching studies was the value of keeping a personal journal in which to record thoughts and feelings. On the 9th December 2000 my first entry reads, "Having finished the Alpha course, except for a get together after Christmas, this seems a good morning to start my journal. Yesterday evening I was able to tell my story… I have changed my life in many ways and today is the start of another phase".

When I started the Alpha course I had no doubt about the existence of God and everything I learned was a confirmation of this. The Alpha course is based on Christianity and much of what I had heard made sense to me and fitted in with my own experience. I was left wondering quite how this would all come together in the rest of my life. I had purchased a Contemporary English Version of the Bible called *Into the Light* (4), which explains what the Bible is about and is written in plain English in a way that is understandable. I decided that if I wanted to take things further, I needed to start reading, and so began at page one of the New Testament and read a few pages each morning and then tackled the Old Testament. It took me over a year to complete this, and I appreciate now that this may not be the best way to read the Bible.

Just before Christmas we spent a lovely week in Tenerife, and were struck by the fact that people celebrate Christmas in a similar way all over the world. They are all celebrating the life of one man, a man who was born into an ordinary family, a carpenter who never travelled far and did none of the things that usually accompany greatness. Yet in three years of preaching, this single man now affects the lives of millions of people around the world. The only word I can think of to describe the power of his achievement is awesome.

We returned from our holiday a few days before Christmas and went to church, and for the first time in my life I felt I was there because I really wanted to be. We were at home for Christmas day and unlike previous years we had no visitors. It was just the four of us, John, Jonathan, Edward and I, and we had a wonderful day, spending the afternoon and evening each choosing our favourite activity or game and playing them together.

The following Sunday John and I went to church again, and both decided that we wanted to make this part of our life. We had our Alpha group get together after Christmas, and as the group seemed quite keen to continue we offered to host some follow up meetings at our house. If you had said to me a few years before that we would be hosting a Christian meeting at our home I would have shook my head and laughed.

We asked Les the vicar at our local church at Great Ness about being confirmed.

The Friday evening Bible meetings at home were open to anyone, and highlighted a vast range of opinion within the broad church of Christianity. Inevitably some of the meetings got quite lively and heated and although everyone respected the fact that we are all entitled to our own opinions and beliefs, there were clearly some very diverse views. On a number of occasions I was quite upset by what was said, and decided that after the Easter break I did not want to be part of these meetings. Having agonised over how to say this without offending anyone, I didn't need to as Adrian had also decided that the meetings had come to a natural conclusion.

My coaching practice was becoming increasingly successful, and I worked at making the most of the opportunities that were presenting themselves. Having completed all the other requirements, I finally tackled the assessment paper. The first question on the paper asked what you believe your role to be as a coach. My answer was to 'challenge clients to formulate their goals, to accept the reality of their current situation, to think through the possible alternatives, and in taking action to achieve their goals and fulfil their potential. Coaching stimulates new patterns of thinking by asking the client questions, which raises awareness and uncovers new learning. A coach guides, not in the sense of an advisor, but as a supporter helping the client to manoeuvre around the obstacles along their chosen path, and by providing encouragement. Coaching enables the client to grow as an individual, and further their personal development'.

I submitted the final assessment paper at the beginning of April. Although many people coach without any formal training, it was important to me to know that I had attained some kind of standard in my coaching. I also felt that being able to say I had a coaching qualification would give me some credibility. My journal is littered with thoughts of knowing that things were about to happen in my new career, and indeed they did!

During the preceding few weeks some of the key trainers in the life coach training organisation decided to go different ways. The trainers who had marked all my previous work had now moved to the UK College of Life Coaching, and so I wasn't even sure with whom I would qualify as a life coach. The outcome was that I sent my final assessment paper to both organisations. I was elated a few days later when I received a personal phone call from the UKCLC examiner to congratulate me, saying that my paper was outstanding. It was a phone call I wish I could have recorded, so that I could have listened again on a bad day! As it happened, the examiner who marked the paper was the lady whose presentation had reassured me at the residential weekend over six months before. To me, her phone call was confirmation of all that I had been working toward, and that I had done the right thing in walking away from the other options that I had been considering the previous year. In my journal that day I wrote that I knew that in coaching I had found my life purpose.

A few days later, I received another phone call this time from a member of the UKCLC administrative staff who said that my name had been added to her list of people to contact, to see if I would like to be considered to write a module for the new life coach training course. I was so amazed to receive such a call, as the examiners ink was hardly dry on my assessment paper. I questioned the lady as to whether my name was on the right list. She assured me that it was, and so I asked her to send me the details. I didn't know what would arrive, as I had never been involved in writing a formal training program, and I had never tendered for a contract like this before. When the details arrived there were a number of topics that I could have tackled, but one topic called out to me – the Listening module.

There was not a lot of time to submit the tender which was to be an outline of the final module, but the ideas came, and I put together a structure for submission. I asked a couple of people for advice on how to go about it, but in the end I did what made sense to me. It made me think a great deal about listening; about all the emphasis on learning to speak when we are young, but no one bothering to take time to teach us how to listen. It made me think about conversations I had held and whether I had listened, and how well I was listening now. It made me go back to all the notes and coaching books, but for such an important subject there didn't seem to be a lot written. What I did know was that to train a person to be a good coach they must learn to be a good listener; in coaching it simply is a key skill.

The deadline for applications passed, and I began to think that it was wishful thinking that I could be a course writer. I had only just qualified as a coach, my background in training was very limited, and I didn't know what was expected in an outline tender. Cynically, I thought no matter how good my efforts were, it would be safer for the UKCLC just to award the contracts to those they knew. To my delight they didn't, and a few days later I had a phone call to say that I had been accepted as course writer for the Listening module. I was so excited, in fact ecstatic!

With great enthusiasm I set about writing the Listening module, and learned so much in the process. It was a wonderful opportunity to explore listening in more depth, and to apply this to my own coaching. Listening is not just about hearing the words that are communicated, it is about being able to hear with all your senses, and when this is done with a depth of understanding the result is truly special. I was very pleased with the fruits of my labours, both professionally and personally, and felt privileged that my work would be used to train and encourage new coaches to develop their listening skills. Although not a qualified trainer, I asked if one day I could present the Listening module on the life coach training course.

Life was becoming very busy again; not only was I writing the listening module, I had also decided to pursue the UKCLC course in corporate coaching, and with some colleagues was planning to set up a 'coaching circle' in Shropshire, where people interested in coaching could get together, all this alongside building my coaching practice.

I was still reading my Bible every morning where possible, and remember how I loved reading John's Gospel, which I have read several times since. I had never really understood the words of the first eighteen verses, which I had heard before and which start "In the beginning was the Word..." but once I did, I felt I found something so powerful, and so beautiful I could read them over and over again. By now John and I were attending confirmation classes with a view to being confirmed together in June.

Adrian had kept in touch, and would call by with various tapes and items of interest. I also kept in touch with Anne from the Alpha course with whom I had felt some connection. I noticed that whenever we spoke she always seemed to say something in the nicest possible way that made me stop and think. We met up several times for a chat before she moved back to Suffolk. Her route to Christianity was so different to mine and yet there were many issues that we discussed, where it was clear that we had ended up with the same conclusions. One morning we shared our beliefs in the need to 'just be and accept', that you find 'happiness in the now', the value of 'contribution', our 'connection with nature', the 'importance of listening' and how 'forgiveness is essential' among other things. I came home and wrote the ideas down in my journal including the title of a potential book – A New Way of Living. It seemed to me that there were many overlaps and similarities between the ideas promoted under the umbrella of personal development and the principles of Christianity and I thought that somehow maybe I could bring them together. Mention personal development and people seem keen to explore, but mention Christianity and there is a definite hesitancy.

I know this feeling of hesitancy. In venturing into spirituality or religious teachings, particularly Christianity, there is a feeling that you might get sucked in to something, be sniggered about behind your back, and of course there is always the danger that you discover something that means you might have to change. I had been the person that was getting along with life perfectly OK, and was quite capable of deciding everything for myself, and I certainly didn't want to get involved in anything else. Of course once my curiosity had taken hold, and I started to think about things and learn more, I realised that rather than a faith being a limitation on your life, it actually enhances it. I could have been told that many, many times, but I wouldn't have believed it because this realisation is one that only comes from the experience.

On June 12th 2001, John and I attended Edstaston Church for our service of confirmation. The Bishop of Lichfield led a lovely service and most of our friends from the Alpha course came as supporters. I could feel the love that Bishop Keith imparted as he put his hand on my forehead, and when I got back to my seat I was overcome with emotion. We had our photos taken by a kind lady who attended the service, and Bishop Keith wrote a few words on both our service sheets, which we kept.

The following day Jonathan celebrated his 18th birthday. I wrote 'he is a lovely lad - I am so proud of him and feel he has a wonderful future ahead'. He did have a wonderful future ahead, albeit shorter than anyone could have envisaged.

Eight – Getting To Grips With Prayer

In some ways our confirmation seemed to bring things to a completion, but in other ways it was the beginning. I continued reading the Bible and read a variety of Christian books. I came to see the Bible as a sort of handbook that was there for reference, guidance and support. I came to see Jesus as a role model who could show us how to get the best out of life through a relationship with God. I started to think about how to go forward, and John and I offered to help with the next Alpha course, which was starting in September.

By this time we had been exposed to all sorts of Christians, and some of the things that had been said didn't fit in with my understanding of what a Christian was at all. It doesn't take long to realise why there are so many wars over religious belief, with all parties passionately believing that they are upholding the word of God. It seems to me that God is God, and no matter what religion you subscribe to, everything comes back to one God in the end. As a life coach the emphasis in my training was to be non judgmental of others, and I decided that I would accept that it is not up to me to judge what other Christians do, they must do what they believe is right and I will respect that, whether I agree or not.

I read some articles written by evangelists, and I found it difficult to think of a God of hell, fire and brimstone; it simply doesn't fit with my understanding. The one I know is a God of Love, not of fear. It seemed to me that fears and threats are more to do with man wanting power over other men, rather than God's power.

We met 'bible bashers' who could quote passages from the Bible to confirm that they knew the answers, but surely what counts is not knowing the answers, but whether you are living them. Even I could see that Bible quotations need to be interpreted according to the culture and traditions of the time, and that there can be different understandings. I wanted to let other people have their ideas and be how they wanted to be and I was happy to listen, but then I wanted to be allowed to go and make discoveries for myself – surely this is the fun of exploring. What sort of an empowering faith could it be that has such rigid ideas that make you feel you cannot explore in case you get to the wrong conclusion?

I wondered whether if I had met some of these people first I would have followed my path.

One of the things that came to light was that if I was really going to develop spiritually I needed to get to grips with prayer. Before reading my Bible each day, I would say the Lord's Prayer and a few words of thanks, but I was not sure that I was going forward. I had made some progress with meditation, in fact I went to a class and was able to apply myself much better, and could feel the value of simply being still. I re-read the chapter in *Questions of Life (2)* about how to pray, which said that many people find it helpful to have a structure to follow. I found the four-part structure really useful, although mine evolved slightly differently into – Thanks to God – Sending love to those in need – Forgiveness for me – Request for help and guidance. Mine lacks a clever mnemonic but I can remember it, and that's all that matters. Having a structure means I don't feel I am rambling, no two prayers are the same, and I can vary the time I spend on each part.

Over the months, by experimenting with prayer, it took on a new dimension. When I thanked God I could feel the presence of God and I could sense my face light up and smiling. There is no conscious effort on my part, it just happens!

In sending my love to friends and people in need, I really started to feel that love was flowing from me.

In asking for forgiveness, I felt at peace. Asking for forgiveness of sins is not about something terrible that I have done, but acknowledging anything which is unloving by way of an action, a word or a thought.

Probably the most wonderful part of prayer has been in my requests for help and guidance. This is not 'please God supply me with this or that', but more along the lines of 'please show me the way, help me to be more like Jesus'. On the whole I don't feel the need to ask for anything too specific, because I believe that I will be given what

I need. The most important part of my prayers is in asking to be filled with the Holy Spirit. In surrendering myself to God and making this request, I can physically feel a sense of being filled. The love, peace and beauty of this are beyond words. To me this is a glimpse of heaven.

In returning to this world from my world of prayer within, I often open my eyes and at first look around with an unreal feeling, as though I am not actually where I am sitting.

When I think back a few years and think of what prayer meant to me then and think about what I have just written, I find it difficult to believe how far along this path I have travelled, and how much I have changed. Daily renewal through prayer has become such an important part of my day.

As I started to make progress with praying I experimented further. In *Questions of Life (2)* there was quite a long section on the gift of tongues, and what to do to receive this gift. It all seemed very straightforward, while in prayer you simply speak to God in any language that comes other than English. I will never forget the day I asked for this gift. As I spoke, my breathing got faster and I felt hot. Physically I felt completely overcome, and I stopped because I was shocked by the immense power I felt. If I had been standing, I think I would have collapsed. I had no idea what to expect, if anything, and in that way this experience frightened me. However, a week or so later I tried this again and found this a very moving and fulfilling experience. Every so often I don't know why, but I feel compelled to communicate in this way.

I have had many kinds of experience while praying, feeling that my prayer was being answered, but there was a particular prayer where I did make a specific request and the answer I got was strikingly immediate. In August 2001 on the way to a meeting in the town I tripped over a piece of uneven kerb in the town centre. I fell directly on to the briefcase which I was carrying and hit my ribcage with some force. Initially I was OK and assumed I was just shaken and bruised. After a while I started having difficulty breathing and I only just managed to drive the car home. I rang NHS Direct for advice and John ended up taking me to A&E. Whether I had broken, cracked or damaged ribs was neither here nor there, as the treatment was the same; basically go home, rest, avoid lifting and take pain killers. I was not best pleased with my situation and spent a month or so struggling until the pain subsided. I got to a point of thinking I had fully recovered when the pains came back again, and I started to get visions of this becoming an ongoing problem. On the second day of this pain, I prayed to God that this pain would go and that it would not stop me from doing what I was meant to do. I can only describe the sensation of the response as feeling like a bolt of lightning, a surge of energy, was striking me. The pain went instantly, and has never come back.

No one has ever shared with me their personal experiences of prayer, and my experiences of prayer have never been shared with anyone until now.

In July, John went to the 'Unleash the Power Within' event in London to hear Tony Robbins and returned equally enthusiastic. John had decided that he wanted to do some serious exercise with a view to possibly running in a marathon. He was in the fortunate position of now having a resident coach available to help him to follow up his goal! He started going out running, but through the coaching he decided that he needed to invest in the right equipment, and he too would get a heart rate monitor, as borrowing mine and sharing our sweat did not appeal to me! One evening he came home with his new purchase and tried it out – his heart rate read 39. To start with we thought the monitor must be faulty and so he tried mine, but it was still just over 40. He made an appointment at the doctors and was told he had high blood pressure and that he must stop all exercise immediately, and do no more than a gentle walk, until it was under control. I have often wondered what the outcome might have been, had we not had our coaching conversation. John has since completed the Great North Run.

I have learnt a great deal from my coaching clients as they have shared their lives with me, the details of which I would not divulge due to the confidential nature of the conversations. The one thing that has struck me though is that no matter what status people have acquired, they have the same inner fears, same challenges and same need to be loved. They think they have a personal weakness, but the fundamentals of life run through us all. I have found it very reassuring to know that while we are all different, we are all the same. I can only assume that the same holds true for spiritual matters.

One specific area of learning, which has been illustrated to me on numerous occasions through life coaching, has been the need to forgive in order to be able to go forward with your life. Life coaching allows people the opportunity to explore their situation, and think through the alternative ways that they can deal with it. Although people inevitably start off with a lot of fighting talk, as they work through the coaching process they seem to work toward forgiveness, apologising or letting go. Deep down it seems everyone really knows how to resolve his or her issues; the difficult bit is acknowledging this and then doing it.

Autumn arrived and with it Edward's sixteenth birthday, followed by John's fiftieth for which I was busily making plans for a surprise get together for a few friends. Jonathan left home to live at his new Hall of Residence in Manchester and start his degree in Computing Science, which had its own mixture of happiness and sadness and brought another chapter of our life to completion.

Jonathan's first trip back home was only a few weeks later for John's birthday and I was so happy to see him striding confidently out of Shrewsbury station. We had a good weekend and I think John enjoyed the surprise get together. The following day in my journal I wrote... 'for the last thirty years everything in my life has been very stable – we have only had additions to the family. Obviously this can't continue, and I think our faith in God will help us to deal with whatever lies ahead'.

Like everyone else we were shocked by the tragic events in America on September 11th, but like everyone else we also know that life goes on albeit differently in the face of any disaster. My prayers went out to those people, but I also thought about the reasons why such hatred is generated and what causes individuals to commit such atrocities. It seemed to me that again society is much more focused on doing something about outcomes, rather than trying to do something about the cause, and in this we all have a responsibility.

By the end of 2001 most of the projects I had been working on in my coaching practice were reasonably successful. I had achieved my goal of presenting the listening module for the UK College of Life Coaching, I had some brilliant feedback on how life coaching had helped my personal clients, and I was working my way through the corporate coaching course. I had helped with another Alpha course, had developed my prayer life, and was working my way through the Bible. Physically I had continued walking and jogging three times a week, and had no real problem keeping to my diet changes. Apart from the painkillers I had taken when I had injured my ribs, I was taking no medication and I never felt the need to return to see the consultant to take up his offer. At last I felt I had found myself.

Nine – On a Spiritual 'Fast Track'

As another new year began, I was just finishing reading a controversial and thought-provoking book called *Conversations with God (5)*. For at least a year I kept coming across references to this particular book and while browsing at the airport just before Christmas it caught my attention, so I bought it. Like many books bordering on spiritual and personal development, there is much common sense contained within; new ideas and lessons to be learned. It didn't necessarily all fit in with my interpretation of things, but I see no problem in that, however it did give me a way of understanding an issue with which I had been struggling.

In my role as a life coach I believe that you create your own future, that you determine your own destiny. Personal experience tells me that this is true, because I have made many plans that I have subsequently turned into reality. I have also seen plenty of clients work through the coaching process and achieve their goals. On the other hand, as a Christian I believe that we are all part of a plan which unfolds, and that the future in this sense is already written. I prayed for clarity on this because I felt very concerned that my Christian beliefs seemed to be in direct conflict with my beliefs about coaching. Reading *Conversations with God (5,)* I realised that seemingly contradictory ideas can co-exist but at different levels, rather in the same way that in an earthly sense I can accept that we are individual bodies, but in a spiritual sense believe we are all part of one body.

I came to realise that we undoubtedly have free will, and to an extent do create our futures. I see our earthly life as the bodily experience where we have the opportunity to create, experience and live. In living we are all moving toward the ultimate goal of fulfilment of our eternal souls, which is through spiritual experience. Watching, listening, and sensing enables us to see opportunities to do this which arise all the time, which we can choose to follow or to ignore. We can live our lives to the full or not, it is up to each individual and there is no right or wrong – this is our choice. There is no short cut; wherever we are up to we have to learn and experience in order to move on, and when we are ready the teacher always appears. Things are revealed to us as we learn, but we don't always take any notice, it is up to us. As a coach I see myself as helping people to become aware and move in the direction that is right for them at that time, and they choose.

At a different level, I can see that in making our individual choices we have an effect on every moment of our own lives, but this also affects everyone else's life. If you choose to go out somewhere, your very presence affects everyone and everything with which you have contact, and creates your and their future. No matter the distance, we are all interconnected to each other and God, and as someone once said – "everything counts", every thought, every word, every action has its own knock on effect. It is an ongoing process which unfolds with time. Decisions that have already been made make the past, which cannot be changed. Every new decision made now has to be based on the previous one, which, once made, determines the future. In this sense you could say that the future was set in motion from the very first decision. At this level, as individuals, we are part of something much bigger and interdependent, and to this extent our future cannot be determined individually. As a Christian, I accept the future as being already written in a way that we cannot fully comprehend.

My faith and my coaching had come together and I firmly believe that the two were meant to be. On February 1st 2002 I wrote 'I know that through the coaching somehow combined with Christianity wonderful things will happen'.

Successful completion of the corporate coaching course was matched with success in gaining contracts with major organisations. Although I enjoyed the work that I did, I felt that my heart was really in working with individuals who were considering setting up their own businesses. Self-employment is an opportunity to take some control over life and offers flexibility, and there are many people that know that this is the direction that they want to move in, but are not sure if they can do it. Running your own business is not necessarily about understanding business, most of it is common sense and you can always learn from books - it is more about understanding yourself. Having had plenty of experience in this area, and some success in coaching budding entrepreneurs, I found that these people seemed to be drawn to me.

In the summer of 2002 I made a decision to promote myself more specifically to those who were setting up their own businesses and called my coaching practice *Going Solo*. This did not mean that I would not coach any other type of client; it was more that it gave me a focus for marketing myself. One of the ways I decided to do this was through the Internet, and I asked Jonathan if he would set up a website for me in the summer holiday. This arrangement worked well because, as a student, Jonathan was looking to earn some additional income. He also wanted to keep in touch with his girlfriend On-in who had returned to Thailand, and the time difference was such that he was looking for any work that left him free in the afternoons. I was delighted with his website design, and he incorporated lots of clever features which make it look very professional, indeed some of my colleagues asked if he might do some work for them too. His handiwork can be seen at www.goingsolo.net. As part of my marketing plan, Jonathan built in a structure to allow me to send out a regular newsletter, which I call an e-guide, to give those running their businesses something to think about! In promoting *Going Solo* I joined various groups and organisations, got involved in more activities, widened my circle of contacts and increased my number of clients.

John and I were actively involved in supporting the church, and having interesting discussions on the role of structured religion and whether it is necessary. For all the criticism that can be levied at organised religion in this country, that it is out of touch and lacks appeal, it still provides much support and is the cornerstone for group worship. Despite the shortcomings, to me there is a significance in sharing Communion that cannot be found elsewhere.

Also during the summer, John and I extended our interest in health issues. Two years had passed since my attendance at the Tony Robbins event and my new lifestyle had become a matter of fact. Healthwise I felt great, however I am always on the lookout for new ideas. We are all familiar with the diverging opinions on what constitutes good health; one week we hear that we should all do one thing, and the next week that has been discredited and something else takes its place. It leads to total confusion, so we all pick out the bits that we want to believe. One of the areas that we did take on board is that, even with a good vegetarian diet, our food no longer contains all the vitamins and minerals that we need to cope with the changing world in which we live. Equally, many products that we buy contain all sorts of additives, the effects of which are largely unconfirmed, and many of which are totally unnecessary. In what we breathe in, rub in, and eat, there is no doubt that we are all being exposed to an increasing cocktail of chemicals. In an attempt to redress the balance we added supplements to our lifestyle and started to choose our purchases, including toiletries and groceries, much more carefully.

In looking into this aspect of health I also became aware of how making a profit for some companies is their only goal, because of the overwhelming need to satisfy their shareholders. There is nothing wrong with making a profit; it is how you do it that matters and integrity seems in short supply. The world is a wonderful place, and there is more than enough to go round, but people are so intent on what they can acquire for themselves. One of the saddest statistics that I have ever read is that there are six billion people in the world, and one billion have no clean water supply. They never will have unless we change our attitude on a big scale and share what we have. As an individual you wonder what you can do, it seems such a hopelessly big task, but really it starts with each person taking a new look at how they live their life and making some changes.

I felt some sense of achievement at having finished reading the Bible from cover to cover, not that I could claim to remember or understand it all. I decided that I wanted to keep reading the Bible, and did this through the daily reading series called *Every Day with Jesus (6)*, to which Adrian had introduced me. I think of the readings as spiritual food. As well as reading books and listening to tapes on coaching/personal development I ventured in to other spiritual/Christian reading, which helped me to further clarify some of my thoughts.

I very much enjoyed an audio series called *Thirsting For God (7)* on the spiritual lessons of Mother Theresa and was struck by the message on what she called her business card which is so beautiful in its simplicity – 'the fruit of silence is prayer, the fruit of prayer is faith, the fruit of faith is love, the fruit of love is service and the fruit of service is peace'. One of these audiotapes was about seeing Jesus in others, in what Mother Theresa describes as a "distressing disguise". Shortly after I listened to the tape this idea was made real to me when I went into Shrewsbury library and, walking down the stairs, saw someone that I didn't know well, but knew instantly the weight of distress that he was carrying. I could very easily have walked by, but I made a point of talking to this person and I was so glad I did because over the following weeks and months we were able to keep in touch. Although I could not change his situation (only he can decide to do that when the time is right) I felt that just by showing him that I cared, I had reached out to this person in a way that I would not have done previously.

As with many things, as you start to investigate to find answers you can end up with more questions. I started to think about other religions and whether they are worshipping the same God but in a different way? I started to think about other spiritual experiences like spirit guides, and how this would fit in with the guide I know as the Holy Spirit? I started to think about the idea that if we have been given free will, did we choose our parents? I have got my own ideas as to the answers to these questions, but have come to the conclusion that although these are great topics for discussion, there never will be definitive answers. The exact nature of belief seems to me to be of minor importance when compared to how you turn those beliefs into the way that you live.

On September 13 2002 I wrote several pages in my journal, the essence of which is captured below and which summarised my beliefs at that time -

'In terms of spiritual experience I sometimes think over the last two years I have got on the fast track – so many things seemed to turn up ….at the beginning of my journey I thought God was the inner most part of each person, and that was it – now I would call that my spirit or soul. My experience has made me sure that the soul is linked to God, the wider universe and thereby to everyone else. I believe that there have been many souls with words from God, but that Jesus *was* the Son of God…that we are all essentially spirits occupying a human body'.

'Joy, love, peace and happiness can only truly be gained by connection with Jesus, God and the Holy Spirit through prayer and meditation...if you follow the teachings of love, kindness and forgiveness in the Bible and live your life as near as you can to Jesus, you can maintain this source of happiness in your everyday life'.

'Jesus came to show us how to live and that bodily death is surpassed by spiritual existence. Not living in the way that Jesus did is 'sinful' in the sense that it takes you away from God. Our purpose is to experience life as individual spirits and in this we have the opportunity to create our future. Others also impact what happens, but we are all part of one. In creating our future we can find what our life purpose is as individuals, and if we live in harmony with our spirit we have much joy...and because we are in tune, we communicate with others in spirit and things happen – nothing is by chance'.

'Suffering is not an act of God, but the result of earthly choices. God is Love and wants us to find our fulfilment and joy with him. God is not angry with us as such, things just are, as humans we can just be, and there is no need to fear...in death spirits who have found peace are given an opportunity to join that eternal existence.'

I had learned a great deal by listening to and reading the thoughts of spiritual writers who are not necessarily Christians, but clearly know God. A conversation that I had with Anne from the Alpha Course made me realise that if you accept that there is only one God, then it is your route to God that counts. I believe that I have been guided by God and shown a true route through Jesus and the Holy Spirit. This route had worked for me and many others, but I have total respect for other views, many of which are based on the same fundamentals of love, kindness, forgiveness and sharing.

One idea that has helped me is to think of life as our perceptual world, one which is continually changing with time. Nothing is the same from one moment to the next, or is it? When you think about the person within, there is something that never changes. If you look in the mirror you are clearly different to a few years ago, but your essence, your soul, whatever you call it, never changes. In fact, it is the only permanent thing that we know as individuals. From this I can only conclude that reality is not actually the perceptual world, the world we see about us, but it is the spiritual world, which can only be accessed from within us. In our earthly life this is the only place to find absolute constancy. Looking at things in this way means that there is nothing to fear in this life, as nothing can really hurt you. If you can recognise the 'you that never changes', regardless of the outside world, you have demonstrated the reality of an eternal being. Having done this, there is every reason to develop your spiritual understanding. It is prayer that links that place within us to the Holy Spirit, to Jesus and to God, which are our best efforts at earthly descriptions of different aspects of this unique spiritual connection.

Over the year I had become more aware of what I can only describe as the rhythms of nature, in that I could sense one phase of life ending and another beginning. Life for me and others seemed to be running in cycles, and I realised that there was no point pushing against the tide. The right time comes for all things. In conversation I often noticed how I would say something, which sowed a seed but that person never picked up on it, and then when the right time came they followed it up. I see this happening all the time, and know I have done exactly the same with many things that have been presented to me.

As part of my role with the UKCLC promoting life coaching, John and I took the opportunity to attend the Vitality Show in Manchester. There were all sorts of weird and wonderful things on offer, some of which I would have laughed at years ago, but not anymore. Maybe the treatments on offer are the result of individuals discovering a particular aspect of God and tapping into those healing properties. Scientific explanation may be thin on the ground, but for some these treatments clearly produce incredible results. One of the stands that I found fascinating was that offering photo–imaging of a person's "aura", the energy field that surrounds us. I had come across this idea before but never had the opportunity to have my photo taken. As well as the photograph of the image, mine was primarily violet; the lady doing this gave her interpretation. From the colours I thought that she described my personality quite accurately, adding that the white colour on one side indicated a divine connection, which I thought was rather interesting. When she looked at my image she asked if I was a writer. I said no, but told her I had often had ideas of writing a book but I had never started because I thought no one would want to read what I had written. She looked at me and said, 'I can assure you plenty of people would like to read what you have got to say'. I walked away from her stand feeling rather pleased with myself and thinking that the website and my e-guide, about which I had not been altogether confident, were destined for real success!

Having lived through some life changing events over the last three years 2002 was a year of consolidation, revelations and understanding. I looked at the world in a very different way and could see how this earthly world is dominated by ego, by want, by being better than the next person and how we languish in all this, in the misguided thought that this will bring happiness. From individual level right up to governments, this is what we do. We are continually exposed to pop stars and celebrities who have got it all, but have lives that are a complete mess, and yet we still persist in fooling ourselves that this is what life is about. Every problem we think we can cure by dealing with the symptoms rather than addressing the root of the problem, which is actually us. The spiritual world is exactly the opposite - it teaches about love, sharing, being equal to the next person and offers eternal happiness and peace. In living by a new set of values and leaving our egos aside, it dawned on me that this is what it means to be "born again" and this is really what life is all about.

Ten – Expecting The Unexpected

The entry in my journal on January 1st 2003 reflects on how happy Jonathan and On-in are, on the pleasure Edward gives us, and on John's love and kindness with the words "I don't think anyone could wish for more". In anticipation of the New Year I have written, "I know things will change and I feel some gaps will occur, but envisage enjoying following my chosen path and loving life, and knowing God at a level which only a few years ago seemed incomprehensible to me". It is impossible to think of the right word to encompass the prophetic nature of this statement.

Relaxing with the Sunday papers at the beginning of the year my eye was caught by what might be in store in the year ahead for Pisces. I have always had a passing interest in reading horoscopes, but more as an amusement than a hobby. I don't know much about astrology or how the interpretations are derived, but I do believe that every thing is connected to everything else, and in this way that the movement of the planets must affect us all. What stuck in my mind was to 'expect the unexpected and that March would be a turning point'. I remember reading this and thinking to myself that things are going perfectly well and I don't want any unexpected events. For some reason this seemed to lodge in my head, and as things happened the word unexpected kept rearing itself in all manner of ways. I have since traced a copy of the New Year horoscope I read and it makes most interesting reading.

Plans were well under way for my parents' Golden Wedding celebration in March, which was being held at our house, when out of the blue we received a phone call to say that Dad had been taken to hospital. He spent about a week there having tests, and I was beginning to think that maybe they would not be able to travel up to Shropshire from Kent. They didn't know it but I had arranged all sorts of surprises for them, including a Rolls Royce.

I also spent several weeks worrying about the possibility of being pregnant. Theoretically this was impossible, but then operations do occasionally reverse themselves. I tried to convince myself that the onset of this unexpected irregularity was simply due to my age, but as time passed I got more worried. John and I put the arrival of

Edward down to an act of God, and I did not want to announce another one.

In the wider world President Bush was waging war and I began to wonder if things would get out of hand, and there would be some terrible catastrophe. Bombs would start dropping in March, and fear and uncertainty seemed to me to be reflected everywhere. War is not the solution, and the many peace marchers show that a lot of people know this. War simply changes the situation and creates a different set of challenges.

Two particularly memorable conversations also come to mind. One was with Adrian about how moved I was reading about bereavement in *Every Day with Jesus (6)* and how the author Selwyn Hughes, who lost his wife and two sons, had found such strength in his belief. The other conversation was with Irene. I had gone to stay in London again for a coaching conference, and somehow we got talking about how your children do not belong to you, but are simply on loan. She gave me a book called *The Prophet (8)* by poet and philosopher Kahlil Gibran which says just this, with many other wise words.

At the end of January I set down in words in my journal how I have come to understand the world. I wrote, "we live in a perceptual world, the world of the mind and body, it is a state of consciousness and dominated by the ego. The real world is one of truth and knowledge and spirit, where we know what is right and don't have to learn. The world of our spirit is part of the kingdom of God, the field of love and energy of which we are all part. Through Jesus' coming we have the Holy Spirit to guide us if we are prepared to ask, but to see this we have to surrender ourselves to God. Until this is done it is simply not possible to reap the spiritual understanding that is there for us all, or to know the beauty, peace and stillness of God's presence".

I also came across a book which Anne and John from the Alpha course had given us when they moved from Shrewsbury called *Find It Fast in the Bible(9)*. I remember looking at this book, thinking I was given this for a reason, and wondering when I might use it. In fact the time was getting very near.

March arrived and we brought Mum and Dad back to stay for the week that would culminate in their 50th wedding anniversary on the 14th March and my birthday and their celebration meal on the 15th March. We had arranged to go and see 'Carmen' at the Manchester Opera House while they were staying, and to call in and see Jonathan and On-in at his student flat at Wilmslow Park for a cup of tea in the afternoon. As a surprise for the celebration on Saturday, Jonathan had been putting together a CD with some of Mum and Dad's favourite music from the 50's, which he had downloaded from the Internet. While we were visiting, we intended to collect the CD so that we could bring it home and make copies for the seven families who would be present for dinner, and which they could keep as a memento of the evening. At the first interval of the performance of Carmen, John received a text message saying that we had forgotten the CD! So at the end of the performance, we had to explain to Mum and Dad that we needed to go back to see Jonathan to collect something. We drove back and I got out of the car and met him outside the flat to collect the secret package - it was the last time we ever saw him there.

We had planned a wonderful day of surprises for Mum and Dad's actual anniversary on Friday 14th March. Flowers arrived; John took Mum and Dad to have lunch with Mum's brother and his wife, and a Rolls Royce decked with gold ribbons brought them back. Pat, Mark and family and Paul, Jannine and family were all here waiting when they returned for tea, and a bit later Mum's other brother arrived.

The 15th March was my birthday and the celebration dinner, which definitely did start off with the unexpected. I thought I would go out jogging as usual, and take some time for myself before all the other visitors arrived and the festivities started. I hadn't gone far when I was badly bitten on the leg by a dog, and had to be driven home. I just couldn't believe that it had to be that day of all days. We had so much to get ready, and all I wanted to do was to sit in a quiet place and rest my leg, but there was no way I was going to let this spoil the big day. I was bandaged up and with a few alterations to the arrangements, the day continued.

John and Mark went in to Shrewsbury to collect Jonathan and On-in from the station, along with glasses and balloons. Preparations continued and by the middle of the afternoon we were just about ready to greet the remaining guests and enjoy the afternoon and evening to come. We had cake and champagne, photos on the patio and a wonderful dinner party with nearly all of our close family. Jonathan's CD was a final touch to what was a perfect celebration.

We said goodbye to some of our guests that evening, but Mum and Dad, Pat, Mark, Paul, Jannine and their families and Jonathan, On-in and Edward were left to reflect on all that had happened. With the number of overnight guests Jonathan and Edward camped together with us in our bedroom.

The next morning was occupied seeing our guests off and clearing up. We had all had such a wonderful time, Mum and Dad couldn't thank us enough for our efforts, and I felt very sad at saying goodbye to all the family. Having waved them off, I walked round the back of the house with tears in my eyes and said to John that I felt so sad because I knew that we would never see all these people together again. Age itself meant that some of the older members of the family would not be around much longer, but I never thought about losing any of the younger members of the family. Jonathan, On-in and Edward helped John take all the tables back to the village hall, and we settled back in the afternoon for a well-earned rest. We had Sunday dinner together in the early evening so that Jonathan and On-in could get the 19.57 train from Shrewsbury back to Manchester. I reversed the car as they said their goodbyes to John and Edward.

We didn't think we had a lot of time, but when we got to the station we discovered that the train would be a few minutes late and went in to the shop so that Jonathan could buy a paper to pass the time on the two-hour journey. I gave Jonathan and On-in a big hug each and we said our final few words – mine were something like 'love you lots, take care, and see you soon'. They boarded the train and I waited on the platform for the train to pull out, but it didn't. Instead another carriage pulled up, and several men converged on the platform at the back of the train, pointing and talking. Jonathan was mouthing to me 'what's the hold up?' and I stood on the platform trying to explain in hand signals what was happening. A few minutes more passed, it was quite cold and I began to think whether I should just go, but something told me that I should stay there and see their departure through. The train continued to wait in the station. Then the new carriage was backed up to the front of the train and after more discussion was finally attached. From Jonathan's responses it was clear that I had managed to communicate with him quite well, and we were all pleased when the train started moving albeit about 20 minutes late. I walked along the platform with the train and waved to them both. I could never have imagined that this was the last time I would see this lovely young man alive. I walked down the station steps with tears rolling down my face and sat in the car crying. As a parent, saying goodbye never really got any easier, but following such a wonderful family weekend it seemed even more difficult.

After all the excitement, Monday was something of an anticlimax and I didn't feel like doing much. Midweek things started to get better and I got a surprise in the post. As a thank you for organising the weekend my sister Pat had sent me Paul McCartney's latest CD. I was thrilled to bits, as in a few weeks we had tickets to see him in concert at Earls Court.

Our arrangements to keep in touch with Jonathan were never fixed to specific days or times, he rang and e-mailed and we did the same on the basis that we would assume he was OK unless we heard differently. John had spoken to him in the week, and I planned to ring him at the weekend. As it happened he beat me to it, and unexpectedly rang us on Saturday evening, while we were all watching a recording of a weekly episode of the Early Adventures of Superman! Jonathan's call was primarily to speak to John about something to do with the computer, but when John had finished, I took the phone for a quick chat. Jonathan told me he had seen the whole Superman series via the Internet, and that the first few episodes were particularly good along with the last ones. He told me that he and On-in had gone to the cinema the night before and that things had not gone according to plan, which included a Chinese lady blurting out random words as the film progressed. He was able to see the funny side of what had happened, including the final straw, which was On-in receiving a strange anonymous text message! Our conversation ended with us having a laugh about life, and we said our final goodbye.

Eleven - Monday 24th March 2003

Monday 24th March was an ordinary morning; I went into Shrewsbury to do some coaching for a local company, and got back the photos from my parents' Golden Wedding celebrations along with a few birthday cards. I went to see the nurse at the doctor's surgery to have the dressing changed on my leg wound as a result of the dog bite, and was late, having got held up in a traffic queue. The last thing I said to the nurse was I would definitely be on time on Friday. Edward was at school and John was at home working.

In the afternoon, I did my usual drive to Gobowen for a piano lesson with the teacher to whom I have been going for years, whose patience with her fumbling pupils never ceases to amaze me. I left there just after 4pm as usual to drive to Oswestry School to pick up Edward and take him back to Gobowen for his piano lesson. Sometimes I go shopping while Edward has his lesson, but on this particular day I had taken some magazines to read in the car while I waited, which is where I was when the mobile phone rang.

It was John. I remember hearing his shaking voice and asking him if he was alright. His response was 'not really'. He asked me if I was sitting down. My first thought was that something had happened to my Dad, but he continued that he had received a call from the Greater Manchester Police to say that Jonathan had been involved in a road accident and had been taken to the Royal Manchester Infirmary. His condition was described as poorly. My heart sank and I started to cry. John said he would ring On-in and ring me back as soon as he knew any more.

I composed myself and decided that even though Edward's piano lesson was nearly over, I must go in and get him and that we should go straight home. I went into the room and as I started to speak could clearly see the anxiety and panic in my voice being reflected back to me in the look on Edward's face. I said we must go, as we would almost certainly be going to Manchester, and Edward drove me home.

When we got home, John had spoken to the police again and been told that Jonathan had serious head and chest injuries – we stood in the kitchen hugging each other and crying. We made a couple of phone calls cancelling arrangements, threw a few things into a bag for an overnight stay, got a drink and decided all three of us should head for Manchester immediately. The last thing I picked up were the photos of my parents' Golden Wedding, thinking that seeing those might help Jonathan recover.

I didn't know what to think on the drive to Manchester; I had visions of seeing Jonathan wired up to machines, of frequent visits to Manchester, of him being brain damaged, of him being pushed round in a wheel chair and that he was dead. The police rang not long after we had set off and said we should go to the police station first and a police officer would escort us to the hospital, then a little while later we had another call saying they didn't want us to get lost going to the police station, to go straight to the hospital and that the police officer would be there to meet us. As I became increasingly anxious, so John kept trying to reassure me. He said he was trying to send Jonathan all his love and strength, and I tried to do the same but it was so difficult.

Ever the practical person, I asked John to stop at the Shell garage on the way in to Manchester to use the toilet, as I knew that once I got to the hospital my only concern would be Jonathan. We drove round the corner and pulled up at the Accident and Emergency Department just before 8 o clock in the evening, not really knowing what to expect.

We walked up to the reception, and announced our arrival. We were asked to wait. A nurse came and asked us to follow her to a side room. On the way we passed On-in, and Jonathan's friends Roger and Vincent, who said nothing, but who were clearly totally distressed. We went into the room and closed the door. I will never forget the first few words the nurse used, which I knew immediately could have no other ending. "There is no easy way to tell you this …."

My mind was a blur of disbelief, of sobbing, of saying 'No God No', of hugging John and Edward; of thinking this is a nightmare it can't really be happening. The emotional pain unleashed was indescribable.

The nurse told us that Jonathan's neck was broken and the spinal cord had been completely severed. There was no way that he could have survived, even though he had been kept alive technically until shortly before we arrived.

By now the police bereavement officer Stuart had joined us and from him and the nurse we started to get an idea of exactly what had happened. Jonathan was using the pelican crossing on Oxford Road, a busy main road into Manchester, near his student flat. A bus had pulled up at the pelican crossing and there was another bus in front at the bus stop. With the green man lit, Jonathan crossed the road between the two buses. A car came speeding past the bus, through the red lights, hit him and drove off. Oxford Road is a busy road, there were already twenty-five witnesses, and the police were looking for a black Honda Prelude. I felt totally numb.

On-in, Roger and Vincent came into the room and shared the pain. On-in loved Jonathan so much it was heartbreaking.

We could hardly believe the nature of Jonathan's death. John has two sisters, Jean whose stepdaughter was killed by a hit and run driver, and Ann whose son Graham was killed in a road accident at the age of 17. Jonathan was born three years later and was named Jonathan Graham after him.

The nurse came and asked if we would like to see Jonathan. Edward said he would rather remember Jonathan as he was, but On-in wanted to see him. I had never seen a dead person before and didn't know how I would cope with seeing my own son, but my overwhelming thought was to support On-in. We all followed the nurse through casualty, Edward waited outside and we took turns with each other to see Jonathan. John and I held hands across him and cried as we struggled to say The Lord's Prayer with him.

Jonathan had a cut on his head, but apart from that he looked to be asleep, just as he did when he was a little boy and I used to go and check on him before going to bed. There was no fear, no anguish, just peace.

Over the next few hours we went to see him several times. Each time we saw him the terrible truth pierced our disbelief that this had happened and could not be changed. While I stood with On-in looking at Jonathan, I said to her I felt that I had lost my son but I had gained a daughter, and I asked her if she would like to be part of our family. I said if she liked she could call me Mum, and she said she would. I knew that Jonathan loved On-in so much that in his absence he would want us to care for her. The significance of this conversation was not revealed to me until two days later.

While we looked at Jonathan I asked On-in what she thought Jonathan might say to her. She said, 'I love you'. I asked her what message he might send. She said, 'Be happy'.

Stuart and the nurse helped us share the pain and did everything they could to support us. We were given two books to look at when we were ready – "When Someone Dies" which had all the contact numbers that we might need, and a Home Office book - "Advice for Bereaved Families and Friends Following a Death on the Road" which explained the criminal side of things.

We started to think about what to do next.

We needed somewhere to stay for the night and decided that the best thing would be to all book into a family room, and for Edward and On-in, John and I to spend the night together. By now it was 10pm and despite Stuart's numerous phone calls, the best option was a double and a twin room at the Travel Inn in the centre of Manchester.

We thought about the devastation we were about to bring to Mum and Dad and our family. We couldn't just make a phone call and we didn't want the police to go round to their homes. In the end we decided that the person to whom we would pass this dreadful responsibility, was my sister Pat's husband, Mark. Initially we tried to ring that evening but couldn't get through, so in the end decided to ring first thing on Tuesday morning.

We didn't know what Jonathan's student room-mates knew, and so rang them and said we would call round to Wilmslow Park on the way to the Travel Inn. We left the hospital at about 11 o'clock having lived through the most traumatic six hours of our lives, and I knew even then that we had only just started the ride on what would be the biggest emotional rollercoaster we had ever been on.

It was a short drive to Jonathan's flat, and when we arrived it was clear the flatmates already knew that Jonathan had died. Very few words were exchanged; it was more hugs and tears.

We got to the Travel Inn and were relieved to find that our double and twin rooms were adjoining. Although we had been supplied with water and tea at the hospital we were all thirsty, and stood alone in the hotel bar at midnight, drinking lemonade before finding our rooms.

We were all so tired, physically, emotionally and mentally, that it was a relief to get to our bedrooms and lie down. Life would never be the same without Jonathan, and I dreaded the agonies that were to come as our personal tragedy became family's, friends' and public knowledge. I don't know if I went to sleep, all I can remember is the next five hours were a mixture of laying on the bed, going to the bathroom, hugging John, crying and thinking. Despite the overwhelming sadness, I started to think that the only way forward was to celebrate Jonathan's life.

Twelve - God So Loved The World

Just after six o'clock John started trying to phone Mark. We didn't know what time he got up, but knew we must catch him before he went to work. Just after 6.30am he finally picked up the phone. I don't think that there is any harder phone call to make, knowing that you are unleashing the same devastation that you have experienced on all your family. It is a phone call none of us will ever forget.

We slowly got ourselves up, and On-in and Edward came in to see us. The sorrow I felt for On-in and Edward is indescribable. It seemed so unfair, none of us had done anything to deserve this, and all our dreams of how the future would be had been taken from us. Added to that On-in and Edward had the pain of turning on the early morning television and Jonathan being headline news.

After nibbling at some breakfast and making a couple of phone calls we left the hotel and went to see Jonathan in the Chapel of Rest. When we arrived, the bereavement centre was full of Jonathan's student friends, many of whom we had never met. We were very touched that they had felt that they had wanted to come and say such a personal goodbye.

When I saw Jonathan that morning I touched his hair, stroked his face, kissed him, put my arms around him and told him how very much I loved him.

Stuart needed to see us to tell us what was happening from the police point of view and said that everything was being done to trace the car. When he said they were using the police helicopter, I started to realise that we were part of a major incident and that we would have to deal with more than Jonathan's death. He also explained that due to the criminal investigation, there would have to be two post mortems and that it was likely that there would be a twenty-eight day delay before we could obtain a death certificate and have a funeral. I just wanted to go home.

On-in's mum wanted to come from Thailand to be with her, and enquired about flights but without any success, and although we wanted to go home we couldn't leave Manchester without knowing that On-in was with someone. We were so grateful that On-in's brother's girlfriend had come straight over from Nottingham and could stay the night.

Leaving Manchester it was difficult to believe what had happened. We didn't know whether we wanted to buy a newspaper or not, but in the end we did. You never think it conceivable that the headlines might be about your own son. On the drive back we decided that we would go home first, and then go round to our close neighbours and friends Rosemary and Bernard, and tell them personally what had happened.

We asked Edward if he would like to see any of his friends. He said he wanted to go and talk to his friends at Oswestry School, which we arranged.

Stuart rang as we were driving back and said that the press were likely to be camped outside the house, and suggested not to deal with them. Apparently they try to obtain photographs that they can then sell on to other newspapers. Seeing a car that we didn't recognise at the end of the drive we didn't stop at home, we went straight to our neighbours, where Rosemary opened the door in floods of tears. We were horrified to find that journalists had already broken our news to them, in their attempt to find out more about us and get a story. We spent an hour talking and then drove the few hundred yards home. On the way we saw our neighbours Ken and Linda, who walked up to the house. They too had been visited by journalists trying to get background information. John wanted to go and get Edward, so Ken went with him and Linda stayed with me, busying herself in the kitchen and dealing with another journalist knocking at the door. We were both so grateful to all our neighbours for being there that evening.

I had already said to John that I must ring Les, our vicar, when we got back, but word had got to him, and when we listened to the answer phone he had left a message. I rang Les that night, and he said he would come down in the morning.

Meanwhile in Kent, Mark had visited our close relatives and it had been arranged that my brother Paul and his wife Jannine would bring Mum, Dad and Ann, John's sister, who would be arriving later that evening. I was looking forward to seeing them all, but the person I wanted to speak to more than any was my sister Pat. When I rang she was in such a quandary between desperately wanting to be here, and her duties as a mother with her two school age children. They were all distraught, particularly David aged 10, who had always idolised Jonathan. It was barely a conversation with us both crying our eyes out, but eventually the thought came that, rather than just Pat, why not just all come here? The next morning Mark, Pat, David and Sarah got in the car and drove up from Kent.

On Tuesday night at about 10pm Paul, Jannine, Mum, Dad and Ann arrived; there were so few words that could give comfort, we just needed their love and hugs and to know that they would share the grief of this tragedy. We went to bed and managed a few hours sleep.

John and I woke up early and spent ages just talking about our feelings. Neither of us felt any bitterness or anger for what had happened. We didn't believe that the car driver had set out that day to kill our son, but his recklessness and irresponsibility had taken our most precious gift. From everything we had read, believed and experienced we knew that bitterness and anger eat away at you, drain you and serve no purpose. It was a route that we decided we did not want to take.

Our spiritual journey had brought us to the belief that as individuals we are eternal spirits, temporarily inhabiting a bodily world and so in a spiritual sense we felt at peace. Given our belief that Jonathan's soul has not died, but has simply moved on to a new experience in his spiritual journey, there is no need to feel bitterness or anger. Conversely, our earthly existence was in tatters, shattered emotionally and physically, with an overwhelming feeling of loss, and so much sadness and sorrow. Having feelings of spiritual peace at the same time as such earthly sadness may seem contradictory, but to us this seemed a natural state to be in.

I tried to pray, but it was difficult to concentrate for more than a few seconds. I thanked God for all that I had, but as I tried to send my love into the world I couldn't as I felt overwhelmed with love directed to me. I had always given in prayer, but today was my day to accept.

Edward had decided that he wanted to go to school and share his sorrow with his friends. Oswestry School has many strengths, but at a time like this its strength is in its community spirit, and we all felt it was the right place for Edward to be.

We were greeted on Wednesday morning by the first of a succession of beautiful flower deliveries. Friends arrived at the house to share the sadness, and some brought us cakes, which we thought was a lovely gesture. We were quite overcome with the kindness and generosity of people some of whom we didn't know well, but whose hearts had gone out to us when they heard our news.

Les arrived and we talked about Jonathan and the pain we were going through. It was a turning point for me when he said, 'Of course God knows the pain of losing a son - he gave his son to the world'. When he said that I suddenly remembered the words that the Bishop of Lichfield had written across the service sheet at our confirmation - 'Read John 3, verses 16 and 17' - "For God so loved the world that he gave his only begotten Son, that whosoever believeth in him should not perish, but have everlasting life. For God sent not his Son into the world to condemn the world; but that the world through him might be saved". I had even brought a little laminated card printed with these words from Lichfield Cathedral for John. It was then I knew that God was with us, and would help us through this tragedy. Les said some prayers with us all. We said we would like someone to come and say a few words with Jonathan in the Chapel of Rest, and although Les kindly offered, we decided to see if a hospital chaplain was available first.

We had arranged to meet On-in at the Chapel of Rest just after lunch, and knew that we may need to leave before my dear sister Pat and her family arrived. I don't know how they did it, but I was so pleased to see them all at midday. Having got out of the car from the 200-mile journey from Kent, Pat had a cup of tea and within half an hour was in the car with us on the way to Manchester.

When we arrived at the Chapel of Rest On-in was with friends from Sheffield, who seemed to have reassured her. Having talked to the chaplain for a while about our beliefs, we all joined the chaplain who was able to use what we had said so beautifully. The words that stuck in my mind were that 'we had welcomed Jonathan into our arms, and now God had welcomed him into his'.

Stuart updated us, and we gave him some information so that a police press statement could be issued as he said to 'pull some heart strings' and encourage people to come forward with information. We also gave him one of our most treasured possessions, a frame with a photo of Jonathan all dressed up for the Valentine's Ball at Oswestry School, which had been standing on our mantelpiece for the last year. This became the official photo for the press. We agreed to meet Stuart the following day at the University Conference centre to put together the statement for the coroner.

On the way home in the car with Pat we talked openly about our beliefs and shared our ideas in a way that none of us had before. In a strange way we all felt better for our visit to Manchester. It became so clear to me that although everyone had come to support us, that by being together as a family we were all supporting each other.

When we returned, Mark had organised dinner. A copy of the Shropshire Star carried the story of Jonathan's death on the front page and it felt so unreal reading back to myself the words that had come to me the day before in the Chapel of Rest, which I had scribbled on a scrap of paper and given to Stuart. "Jonathan was all you could ever wish for in a son. He had a beautiful girlfriend and everything in life to look forward to. Our whole family and his friends are completely devastated by his death". In the evening we sat looking through and opening all the wonderful cards and letters that had started arriving. This became something of a nightly ritual that we wanted to give time to, and do together. The kindness of people was overwhelming; it was as though the worst in tragedies had brought out the best in people. We had never thought about how many lives our Jonathan had touched until now.

Thirteen – The Way Things Were Meant To Be

Each night I was gradually getting a little more sleep, and on Wednesday night slept until about 4am when my crying made it impossible to lay down any longer. I went into the bathroom and sobbed. I was still thinking about God understanding how I felt, and wondering how I could find support. For some reason I suddenly thought about the passage that I was meant to be reading at St. Andrew's Church at Great Ness on Sunday. John and I are on the rota, and were meant to do the readings in February, but due to a visit to the Lake District we had swapped to the forthcoming Sunday, which also happened to be Mother's Day. I had looked at both these readings a week or so before, thinking that I had better agree with John which one I would read, and which he would read. I distinctly remembered that when I had read them, one had really appealed to me and the other didn't seem to say much, in fact I remember thinking what is the point of this? So, in a rather selfish way, I intended to say to John that I would like to read from Colossians, if he would read from John's gospel.

Sitting on the bathroom floor that night I couldn't remember what either reading was about, but just felt I must look at that reading from Colossians 3 vv 12-17 and read:

"God loves you, and has chosen you as his own special people. So be gentle, kind, humble, meek and patient. Put up with each other, and forgive anyone who does you wrong, just as Christ has forgiven you. Love is more important than anything else. It is what ties everything completely together. Each one of you is part of the body of Christ, and you were chosen to live together in peace. So let the peace that comes from Christ control your thoughts. And be grateful. Let the message about Christ completely fill your lives, while you use all your wisdom to teach and instruct each other. With thankful hearts sing psalms, hymns and spiritual songs to God. Whatever you say or do should be done in the name of the Lord Jesus, as you give thanks to God the father because of him"

I cried and cried as I read this passage over and over again. It seemed to have such relevance to what had happened, and held a message of reassurance that I needed to read.

Then it occurred to me that maybe there was some relevance to the other reading, which had previously seemed to say so little to me. When I read John 19 vv 25-27 I could hardly believe what was written.

"Jesus' mother stood beside his cross with her sister and Mary the wife of Clopas. Mary Magdalene was standing there too. When Jesus saw his mother and his favourite disciple with her he said to his mother, 'This man is now your son'. Then he said to the disciple 'She is now your mother'. From then on, that disciple took her into his own home."

Just two nights earlier I had stood with On-in at Jonathan's bedside, and had said to her that although I had lost a son I felt I had gained a daughter. I had asked her to become a part of our family and she had accepted. In these readings I found the confirmation of faith that I needed in these hours of darkness. I knew that God was guiding me through this suffering, and understood.

These readings had been set months ago, and we had chosen to change dates to the forthcoming Sunday. I had no doubt that we were meant to read them. I know how desperate I felt before I read these readings, and I know the myriad of feelings that I felt after I read them. Although it was so very difficult to accept, I started to feel that this is the way that things were meant to be.

As I shared this story with John and later with Pat, and then with family and close friends I became more certain that in some way this suffering was destined to be part of my life. What makes a whole set of conditions occur which sometimes result in disaster and other times nothing? If Jonathan had left a few seconds later…if the car that hit him had been driven slower…if the bus had not been at the crossing….if… Everyone was going about their lives, making the choices that finally brought so many uniquely timed incidents, all irrelevant in themselves, together in that one millisecond to produce a tragic outcome. Many years ago I had stopped to help at a road accident on the A5 when a workman had stepped into the path of a lorry. I had thought then about how things happen, and how everything comes together in a single moment. I had even talked to Jonathan about the workman, when I was teaching him to drive, to remember that one moment's lack of concentration or foolishness can render horrendous consequences that have to be lived with forever.

I do not know why my family and I might be the ones to carry this burden of suffering, except that someone has to. God is the God of Love and I do not believe that he wants us to suffer; neither do I believe that I am being personally punished. God has not brought about our suffering, except in the sense that he gave man free will and in allowing this it is man, through his separation from God, that makes his choices and generates suffering. All the while people remain separated from God, their spiritual home, and from the crucial understanding that love is all that really matters, disasters, tragedies and suffering will be the inevitable consequence. Suffering is the sad outcome of man's chosen way of living, and even though this lesson is demonstrated continuously, we are too blind to see and learn. Jesus suffered at the hands of man's free will, and some of us will inevitably be chosen to share the experience of this suffering with God. Rather than take away my belief in God, these events have served to strengthen it.

I believe that in Jonathan's short life he fulfilled his purpose, that in some way his earthly life was complete. Out of this tragedy good will come, because all those moved by his death will, to a greater or lesser extent, re-evaluate their own situations and think about what is important in this world. Although we may not be able to understand, I am sure that Jonathan's fulfilling his purpose will, in some way, help us and others to move closer to fulfilling theirs.

Fourteen – 'The Best Times Of My Life'

On Thursday morning we had arranged to meet Stuart at the Conference Centre to do the statement for the coroner and had taken Mum and Dad with us to Manchester. Stuart told us that the car had been found, albeit partially burned out and had been taken for forensic investigation. We spent several hours providing details of Jonathan's life.

The Registrar and the Vice chancellor of UMIST took time to see us, and we were able to express our concern for On-in and said that we would like to do something to celebrate Jonathan's life within the University, although we were not sure what.

In the afternoon we went to the Chapel of Rest with Mum, Dad and On-in who had brought some of the letters and cards and emails that Jonathan had given to her. I had told many friends that Jonathan was in love, in fact I had often used the word besotted, but that afternoon we were about to find out a beautiful side to our son that we never knew.

On-in told us that Jonathan had arrived late for his first lecture in September 2001 and there were only a few seats left at the front. She said he turned round and their eyes met. His friends have told us that he never stopped talking about this girl he had seen, and they got fed up of encouraging him to speak to her, or to make contact in some way. It took him until February 2002 to build up the courage to do something - he bought a Valentine card.

On-in showed us the card. On the envelope he had written one word – Beautiful – and inside he wrote 'for the past few weeks I have seen you in lectures and thought to myself "How could I ever get to spend time with a girl so beautiful, clever, sweet and fun?" I wanted to speak to you before, but I never had the words to say, so now it is Valentine's Day I decided to give you this card. I was hoping you might like to go for a drink with me one day, or just let me sit with you in lectures sometimes. You would make me the happiest guy on earth if I could see you more, so please call or email me. With love Jonathan'. On-in replied with an e-mail.

Exactly one year later he wrote, 'this time last year I was so scared to give you your card, but I am so glad, because since that day I have had the best times of my life. I want to be with you forever, so expect your Valentine's card every year from now on☺. I love you so much, Jonny.'

We all shed tears at reading these cards. They were tears of joy that Jonathan had found such love, and tears of heartbreak for On-in at what she had lost. As a boy we had given him our hearts and as a man On-in gave him hers. I learned something from Jonathan that day, that instead of trying to find a card that said the right words it was so much better to write your own.

I can have no regrets about Jonathan going to Manchester. It was where he wanted to be. He loved the accessibility and the excitement of the city, and he told me he was sure that Computing Science was the course for him. He had made some great friends, and he was madly in love with On-in. His life was wonderfully full, and he was so very happy.

At the pelican crossing where Jonathan was killed, students and friends had been leaving flowers. We decided that we would go to the flower stall and leave some flowers there too. Amid a busy Friday afternoon John and I, Mum and Dad, On-in and her brother and his girlfriend tied our flowers to the railings, and stood and looked at the spot where Jonathan was killed. Strange though it sounds, I just felt I had to complete the walk across the crossing for him, and so John and I walked across together. As we returned a bus pulled up at the crossing, just as it had for Jonathan, and walking into the road I felt sure that Jonathan would literally not have known what hit him. With the green man showing, there was no reason to expect that a car would be speeding past the bus. How I wished I could have turned the clock back.

We returned to Shrewsbury to another evening of opening cards and making phone calls. The cards and letters were very moving, many of them describing memories of Jonathan. One which I particularly remember reading, and which seemed to capture it all, was from one of Jonathan's teachers, now retired, who wrote 'he was one of the best-natured and likeable boys I came across in twenty one years at Oswestry School, and that is how we shall always remember him'.

As what had happened started to sink in, it became harder and harder to make the necessary calls to our friends. It is such devastating news to land on anyone. There was such disbelief, and no one knew what to say, because there was nothing you could say. The shock waves could almost be felt stretching out from us.

Edward did not want to go to Manchester again, but wanted to talk to his and Jonathan's friends. He met up with Chris, one of Jonathan's best friends from Oswestry School, who, like the rest of us, just could not believe this had happened. Chris wanted to say his goodbye in Manchester, and so we arranged for him to come with us the next day.

That night, just before going to bed, John had been talking to Pat and David about beliefs, and Pat had shared a story about a robin she had seen just after a close family member's death. She felt that the robin was there as a message of reassurance of the eternal nature of our spirit, and in times of trouble the robin had often appeared. Pat had never shared this story with anyone before, but when John came up to bed and told me, I remembered the magpie that had appeared after my grandfather's death. I specifically recall this magpie sitting and looking at me, as though he was trying to convey a message. We have lots of birds visiting our garden but I have hardly ever seen a magpie, and I wondered whether a magpie would appear. Since sharing this story three other people have told me of the significance to them of a special bird that appeared. I am sure there are many people who have experiences like this, but never share them because it sounds so crazy to the outside world.

Every day since Monday had been spent in Manchester, and we decided that after Friday's visit we would spend the weekend at home. On the way to Manchester that day a magpie flew in front of the car and did so on several other occasions, each time appearing nearer to home.

Stuart had got Jonathan's belongings, and had written up the statement for the coroner for me to sign. As On-in had been the last person to speak to Jonathan she had to give her statement. They had been shopping at Sainsbury's together, and had been arranging to meet up with their friends Roger and Vincent for dinner. As Vincent was not sure how to find his flat at Wilmslow Park, Jonathan had offered to meet him outside the BBC building on Oxford Road. He told On-in he loved her and left. A while later she had a call from Vincent to say that he was waiting but that Jonathan had not arrived. This was followed by a call from Roger asking On-in if she knew what was happening as Oxford Road was closed and there were police everywhere. On-in was just on her way out to search for Jonathan when John rang, to say that he had had a call from the police, and that Jonathan was in the Royal Manchester Infirmary.

There was one other thing that I wanted to do before we left Manchester. When both Jonathan and Edward had their first haircuts I had kept a lock of hair, and I just felt that I wanted to keep a final lock of Jonathan's hair. I was concerned that the staff at the Chapel of Rest might consider this to be an odd request, but their response suggested that it was not particularly unusual, indeed they were willing to assist in any way they could. The mortician took On-in and me into the Chapel of Rest and cut two locks of hair, which we put into brown envelopes.

Chris, On-in, John and I said our goodbyes for the weekend, collected On-in's weekend bag and drove back to Shrewsbury.

On-in said that she would like to stay in Jonathan's room while she was with us. I made a point of going with her when she took her bag upstairs, as I felt it would be so difficult for her with all the memories that his room held. I knew that she must have hugged Jonathan in that room many times, and as we were standing talking I saw Jonathan's old teddy bear. I remember buying the bear for Jonathan over twenty years ago, before he was born and he took him to bed every night until he moved to University. I felt so sure that Jonathan wanted On-in to have his teddy bear that, on the spur of the moment, I offered her this most precious bear. The bear had given Jonathan great comfort and I felt sure it would do the same for On-in.

The weekend saw a flurry of activity as Pat and family and John's sister Ann left, and Paul and family arrived, and we tidied up the house.

Fifteen – The Final Goodbye

On Sunday morning Edward presented me with a lovely Mother's Day card and a big box of Maltesers, for which I have something of a soft spot. On-in had written in the card that Jonathan had already bought for me, 'Mum. Thank you for all the love you have given us. Love from Jonathan and On-in'. I will treasure this card forever.

It was so important to me to go to Church that morning. Although John and I had asked Les to arrange for someone else do the readings, I wanted to hear them read, they held such enormous significance. Mum, Dad, Jannine, Edward, On-in, John and I set off for the communion service knowing that in a few weeks it would be where Jonathan's funeral service would be held. It was just a few weeks before Easter and I knew this would not be easy, but I just had to be there. The first hymn was 'Come Down, O Love Divine' - there was no way I could sing through the tears. However, hearing the readings gave me an inner strength, and somehow seemed to bring things together and complete a circle.

It was nearly two years since I had taken part in the communion for the first time, but the importance of this act today in confirming my faith was of infinite magnitude. I knelt at the altar rail with John and as I struggled to swallow the mouthful of wine, I broke down and wept. As I stayed there with my head on my crossed arms and John's arm around me, I sensed the congregation continuing to take communion around me, but I just couldn't move. Eventually I slowly gathered myself together and walked back to the pew for the remainder of the service.

On Monday morning we headed back to Manchester with On-in with a very important task. David, our nephew, had asked if I could put some tulips he had bought in Jonathan's memory at the pelican crossing. All by himself he had written the most beautiful words saying that he would always remember Jonathan, and referring to all the fun that they had had playing Lego. Jonathan was something of a hero to David, who is nine years younger, and I was very moved by what he had written and that he had asked me to do this on his behalf.

A week had passed and we decided to go into Manchester for lunch and start to tackle some of the practical tasks that needed to be done. The first place we called was the travel agents. Jonathan had rung me a month or so before, saying, 'I am outside the travel agents and am going to purchase a ticket to fly to Thailand with On-in on June 30th – is there any reason I shouldn't go?' I said there was none that I could think of, and he laughed when I joked back - 'is it a one way ticket?' The Chinese travel agency was a hive of activity that afternoon, and listening was not one of their strengths. I explained what had happened and that we needed to cancel the ticket. The assistant went away from the desk and when she returned asked me where Jonathan was now. We all stood speechless and just looked at each other, until I finally said he was at the mortuary at the hospital. At this point the poor harassed assistant did get the picture. All I could think of was the 'dead parrot' sketch out of the Monty Python series, and how difficult telling people was obviously going to be. We headed from there to the HSBC to try and sort out Jonathan's bank account and although the lady there couldn't actually cancel his accounts because we did not have a death certificate, the staff bent over backwards to be helpful.

We also called in to the Department of Computation at UMIST to see Jonathan's tutor and Professor McCauley, and as we parked the car commented what a shame it was that this was the nature of our first meeting. We talked with them for about an hour about supporting On-in through the difficult period ahead, and about the possibility of a University Prize in Jonathan's memory, and as a celebration of his life.

I had decided that I should put my coaching clients, and all my work commitments on permanent hold until after Jonathan's funeral, however as we are both self employed one of us needed to earn some income. On Tuesday John said he would go back to his contract at Walsall for a few hours and break the ice, which he did. It was the first time we had been apart for over a week, and he didn't really want to go, but felt he had to. I was so glad when he returned.

Dad's brother Frank and his wife Irene had arrived on Tuesday and they came with us on Wednesday to Manchester to see On-in and to visit Jonathan in the Chapel of Rest. As with everyone else who had been to see Jonathan, they too said that there was a sense of peace about him. We knew from previous conversations that Frank and Irene recognise the importance of finding a spiritual path, and I wanted to share my story about the church readings and my thoughts with them. Irene said she had never met anyone with such faith. The next morning she rang her daughter and told her that she loved her.

The responses that I had received from friends when I had shared my thoughts were a mixture of inspiration, delight and amazement. On Thursday morning, just ten days after Jonathan's death, I felt empowered to start writing some of the phrases that I might share with people. I spoke to my friend Julie who said 'I told you you would write a book one day!' On Saturday 5th April I started typing. I thought that in the first instance just getting everything out of my head and on to paper would be therapeutic. I am sure this is the case, and simply regaining some focus was useful. After typing for a week, I was certain that I must complete this manuscript. I decided that whether what I had written and was about to write was simply read by a few friends, or whether it would be of wider interest really did not matter. I was certain then, as I am now, that when the time comes God will guide me.

We had discussed the fact that at some point we would have to make a practical decision, draw a line, and pay our final visit to Jonathan in the Chapel of Rest. It was Friday, twelve days had passed since Jonathan had died, the University term was at an end and we had arranged to bring On-in back to Shropshire for the Easter break. I felt that Jonathan had moved on and that we must too, and so that morning I asked John if he would phone the hospital chaplains, and ask if someone would come and say a few final words.

We arranged to be at the Chapel of Rest for the last time at 2.30pm and asked if the chaplain could be there at 3pm. When he arrived he said very little and seemed somewhat uncomfortable, but we all went in to the Chapel of Rest and stood by Jonathan with the chaplain on one side of his body, and On-in, John and myself on the other. I can't remember what he said, but after a few minutes he sat down and as he put his hands near Jonathan I noticed he was shaking. I didn't know what was happening, but I started to feel quite frightened. I was paying more attention to the chaplain than to Jonathan, and as John asked him if he was alright the poor man started to keel over. John ran round Jonathan's feet and caught him before he hit his head on the floor. I ran out and rang the emergency bell. It was an awful experience for all concerned. On top of everything else we really didn't need this. I was left shaking all over, and John just kept saying this is not how it was meant to be.

The chaplain recovered and offered to come back into the Chapel of Rest, but I declined. There was no way that I wanted to be left with an extension of this experience as a final memory of seeing Jonathan, and I asked if a different chaplain could come. As we sat wondering what would happen next, John commented that the Chapel of Rest must have looked like a scene from Father Ted, and we thought that at least Jonathan would see a humorous side to this. We were all deeply upset, and went to the Bereavement Centre where the staff made us a cup of tea while we waited for another chaplain.

The new chaplain arrived and we started again. It was difficult for everyone, but she was lovely and found just the right words, reading 1 Corinthians 13 about love, and saying such meaningful prayers. As I stood between John and On-in I remember feeling that my whole body was glowing. It was a sensation of simply being filled with God's love. When the chaplain had finished speaking I put my arms around Jonathan and said 'I love you so much' I drew a cross on his head and said 'Be at peace'. I kissed his beautiful face for the last time and told him 'I will be with you again one day'. I took my last look at him, turned around and walked away with my tears flowing. At peace in the Chapel of Rest is the final memory I have of my dear son.

It had been such an intensely emotional afternoon. We went round to the flat and collected On-in's suitcase and said goodbye to Manchester. When we got back to Shrewsbury there was just

Edward and Chris waiting for us, as temporarily all our visitors had gone, although Mum and Dad were coming back on Sunday.

I was so disturbed by the unfortunate events in the Chapel of Rest that afternoon, that I spent days thinking about what had happened, and spoke to a number of people. I have my own thoughts on what took place. In the end, I came to the conclusion that for whatever reason, and I thought of many such as illness, a test of faith, even that the right person had to be there – we ended with the right outcome. Although it was difficult, I know that I did the right thing in insisting that we start again. I decided that I must focus on the memory of the final goodbye, which was so right. Being unable to understand the reason for what happened in the Chapel of Rest, I took my thoughts to God in prayer, and asked him to cleanse my soul.

Sixteen – As Free As A Bird

We gradually started to get back to doing normal things like going shopping and tidying up the house. I muttered about the bird mess outside the conservatory and on the patio. John commented it was no ordinary bird; it must have been the pheasant that several people had mentioned. Although it was an unusual bird to have in the back garden, I had not really taken much notice. However, on the Sunday morning I could hardly believe what I saw. There was the pheasant, and his mate, standing a few feet from the lounge patio doors, just looking at them. The curtains were closed, and yet the pheasant looked so much as though he wanted to see in, that after a while I felt compelled to go downstairs and opened the lounge curtains for him! He stood and looked at me from the new little patio garden that John had recently finished making, which we said we would plant up as Jonathan's garden. He then walked up to the playroom and just sat and looked at the wall, and then along to the office door and sat and looked at that. I went and got John who had been in the shower, and we stood in the conservatory and watched in amazement as this strange behaviour continued for what must have been another half an hour. Through the pheasant it seemed to me that Jonathan's spirit had found a messenger. I felt sure that the pheasant was Jonathan's way of communicating that although he wanted to be near us in body, his spirit was as free as a bird.

Peculiar though it seems, the pheasant had given me such reassurance that I thought I would tell Edward and On-in what we had seen, even though I expected that they would fall about laughing and tell me that I was being really silly. They were doing something on the computer when I asked them if either of them had seen any unusual birds in the garden, as I had a very strange tale to tell. On-in responded straight away that she had seen a big coloured bird, but she had never seen one before and didn't know for sure what it was. I told them what John and I had seen that morning. To my delight and amazement, On-in told us that late the previous afternoon she was sitting on her own in the conservatory when one of the pheasants walked right up to the doors and just sat and looked at her. Ridiculous as it seems, it made me so happy my heart lifted. In bringing his message of reassurance, the pheasant had joined Pat's robin and my magpie!

That morning I put my new Paul McCartney CD on and sang. I had been undecided as to whether I should even go to the forthcoming concert that I had booked months before and had been so looking forward to, but, mad as it might sound, seeing the pheasant somehow made it possible for me to believe that I could enjoy life again.

I rang Pat to tell her about the pheasant and she told me that she had seen him in the shadows of the oil tank while she was here and had told Mum. When Mum arrived she said that she too had seen him walking along the patio looking into the house. In the same way that Jonathan might have responded to my efforts at the computer, I could hear him saying with some frustration - 'For goodness sake Mum, you are slow! I have been trying to let you know for over a week that although I have moved on, I am fine, and it has taken you all this time to realise'. There is no way that Jonathan will communicate with us again in body, so what better way could be chosen than through an unusual and most beautiful bird.

A reading that we had at church one week about man's inability to listen and see anything further than the blindingly obvious and logical came to mind again. The gist of it is that God tried communicating first by telepathy, but man chose not to hear it. He then tried to communicate by the written word through the prophets, but man chose not to read it. In desperation he finally decided to communicate in person and sent his own son, and he had to die in the effort, but at least he did get the message across. I am sure that there are many diverse ways that God uses, including pheasants, to communicate with us, but sadly we often choose to overlook and ignore them.

With the news that the coroner had decided to release Jonathan's body and that we could now arrange a funeral another phase began. The date would be almost twenty-three years to the day when we were in Kent at Graham's funeral.

The pheasants were frequent visitors to the garden, and we watched them for hours. John and I also saw a magpie on the fence. When all the visitors had gone it seemed the magpie chose his time to arrive. He flew over the house as I opened the curtains one morning and as I went back into the bedroom John said to me, 'Look the magpie is talking to the pheasant!'. There they were, sitting together in the back garden on the bank of plants that Jonathan had helped plant, within a few feet of each other!

Due to Easter we had about ten days to get organised for Jonathan's funeral, which was on the 24th April, exactly one month after he died. We had a couple of meetings with our vicar Les and agreed what we would like to include, although much of it seemed to choose itself. We tried to let everyone know the date, and in the process got in touch with people to whom we hadn't spoken for years. We received many beautiful letters and cards with words of kindness, which gave us hope, including one from the Bishop of Lichfield who had confirmed us.

We went to Kent for Easter and saw the family, and although it wasn't easy, we did go to see Paul McCartney in concert.

On the morning of Jonathan's funeral I reflected in my journal how, just a month before, our life had been reasonably uneventful, and how I wished it could have stayed that way. I would have given anything to change that fateful day, but I knew I couldn't. I loved Jonathan so much, and always will. Such a lot had happened over the last month and yet I had done nothing – my life had just come to a grinding halt. In my prayers that morning I asked God to take me to heaven. I felt my spirit dancing with Jonathan's in pure happiness and delight. He could be anything, do anything, go anywhere – Thailand for him was just a flicker away. For us, such a visit would have to be made in bodily form!

I knew that we were in many people's prayers that morning, and I asked God to give us all strength and to show us how to go forward. I felt certain that in some way this was how things were to be, and could see that in Jonathan fulfilling his purpose we would fulfil ours. I had re-read Selwyn Hughes' thoughts on bereavement in *Every Day with Jesus (6)*, that just a few months before I had discussed with Adrian, and I wrote those observations in my journal –'know that grief will come to you, be prepared and willing to feel it. If you face a feeling you are in charge of it.' Difficult though it is, I know he is right, and I decided to take these words of wisdom with me.

Friends started arriving at lunchtime, and others made their way directly to Great Ness Church. Finally there was just Edward, Onin, John and me left to accompany Jonathan on his last journey. As we drove out of the drive in the pouring rain we laughed about Jonathan accelerating round the corner, and making the shopping slide across the boot of our old estate car, and wondered if the flowers were firmly secured.

As we followed the coffin down the aisle to the sound of "Morning has Broken", I never looked around, just straight ahead. The tributes by my sister Pat and by Jonathan's friends Chris, James and Adam were heart-warming and as the service went on, I felt as though I was getting stronger and stronger. As we walked out of the church, I looked around and realised just how many lives Jonathan had touched. We stood at the church gates, hugging what was an endless stream of people from all corners of our lives. We eventually made our way to the crematorium, and family and friends each laid one of nineteen red roses on Jonathan's coffin. Adrian read the poem 'Please Believe These Words' from a little book called *From Black and White to Colour (10)* with such incredible feeling. Many people commented on the service, and what a beautiful occasion it was. My friend Anne summed it up for me in some words she had written about the atmosphere in the church - "that death was all used up, and love filled every space".

Seventeen – A Message From The Lord

Having all come together on that wet Thursday afternoon, everyone left to go their separate ways. Family and friends said their goodbyes and promised to be in touch. On the way to the station with On-in on Friday, we went to the crematorium and collected all the lovely flowers – our floral 'guitar' went up to the church and decorated one of the windows, On-in's 'heart' was brought home, and we took some of the sprays to the hospice. On Sunday, the last people to leave were Mum and Dad, who had spent virtually the whole month here supporting us in whatever ways they could. When everyone else had gone we were left – John, Edward and I, and the pheasant that would make regular appearances, spending at least an hour in the garden just wandering round with his mate.

By the end of April we had to, and indeed needed to, get back to the business of living. John had decided that he would spend more time working from home, and had plenty to keep him busy, Edward went back to school, On-in was back at University, and I thought about how to get going again with my life coaching. I am not the same person I was, and for me it was not a case of just going back and picking up where I left off on the 24th March. The only two things that I really wanted to do was to write this 'book', and make contact with and get back to coaching my current clients. I didn't want new clients, to promote myself, to be a part of any organisation, or in the public arena, I just wanted time to think, to be left alone, to be with me.

As I got back to various everyday tasks, I had no doubt that I could feel Jonathan's presence in the house, when I was jogging and elsewhere. I had to turn round and look at the back passenger seat of the car one day, I was so sure he was there. Of course there was nothing physical to see. I really felt that Jonathan had been confused by his sudden exit from life, and that he wanted to be around to help us all get used to the process of moving on.

The pheasants ceased visiting, but the magpies set up home in the trees opposite our house and I see them frequently when I look out or go out. I have no doubt that there is an element of the 'new car syndrome' that once your awareness is raised you see lots of the same. I also know that there wasn't a magpie to be seen for weeks when I first started looking. It is as though they were drawn here, so that once everyone else had gone, they would be around.

Over the weeks I have survived various 'firsts', like going to a meeting, coaching a client, and returning to piano lessons, but anyone who has suffered such a loss knows it is not easy, and there are good days and not so good days. There was information about the police investigation to deal with, and we were trying to support dear On-in as she started to pick up the pieces of her life, while living just a few yards from where it all happened.

In the middle of May I wrote that in my prayers I felt that God was telling me he had chosen me, exactly for what I didn't know. Over the years I have had a recurrent interest in looking into some form of healing, but never followed it up. The Sunday service at Church recently was about vocation, and made me think again about how I am meant to go forward. A recent conversation with a spiritual friend made me think she also knew that I have a task to complete. The daily Bible reading, with which I am several months behind, was focusing on the Servant Songs and the reading for the 24th March is about the servant telling his own story, which starts before his birth.

On May 24th exactly two months after Jonathan died I completed the first draft of this manuscript. On that day I started reading a book that John had given me for Christmas called 'How to know God (11) by Deepak Chopra. We have listened to a number of his audiotapes and found them fascinating. I have never read anything like this book before, which draws insights from all religions and sets out the stages of spiritual growth. The timing of my reading couldn't have been more perfect, as so much of what I had written seemed to fit in with what he was saying. I was glad that I hadn't read it before.

Last week we were preparing ourselves for another phase of activity. We spoke to the school chaplain and finalised the content of a Service of Thanksgiving for Jonathan to be held at Oswestry School on June 21st. We went up to Manchester on Saturday, and cleared out Jonathan's room and bought back his belongings. We brought On-in back with us to stay until she flies back to Thailand for the summer. This week we will be attending the ash burial and then on Friday 13th June it would have been Jonathan's twentieth birthday. Eleven weeks have now passed, and I am sure I will be able to tell you the number of weeks since the Monday 24th March 2003 for the rest of my life.

On Sunday morning, John and I went to church as usual and as we were walking along the road John asked me when the 'book' would be finished. I replied that I thought it would be ready to read by our holiday at the beginning of July, but I hadn't understood the question he was asking. He meant at which milestone would the 'book' be finished, and of course I didn't really know. In Church that Sunday we were celebrating the day of Pentecost, which is when the Holy Spirit descended on the disciples and they received the spiritual guide that they had been promised. I got terribly emotional, and knew that the whole congregation was aware of me sobbing. I recovered myself, and a few people came and spoke to me, but I never thought any more about it until later that afternoon.

A car pulled up on the drive at about 5 o'clock, and much to my surprise it was a member of the morning congregation. She came in and said that she had a message for me from the Lord, that she has received messages before, and felt absolutely compelled to deliver it to me. She came to tell me that during the service some words came to her, which my sobbing indicated were intended for me. The message was that the Lord will carry you, not in the sense of simply supporting, but in the sense of carrying you forward. She said she could not interpret exactly what this might mean. No one has ever given me a message like this before. I find the idea awesome that someone is so empowered that they know they must get in their car and go and deliver a message of this nature to a person that they don't know very well at all. It is not every day that someone arrives on your doorstep with a message from God, but nothing surprises me anymore.

In the evening I decided that I must ring Adrian about the Thanksgiving Service in memory of Jonathan, but in fact I had forgotten we had spoken about it on a previous occasion. He said that as it happened there was something that he wanted to ask me, but had been going to leave for now. Just after Jonathan's death I had told Adrian about the relevance of the church readings, and he asked if he could share my story, which he had done on a number of occasions. In doing this he was asked to ask me if I might like to share my story personally at the Shropshire Prayer Breakfast to be held in November. I have never been asked to make a contribution like this before, and I couldn't help but make the connection between what I had been told that afternoon, and his request. With a sense of disbelief, I even asked him if he had spoken to my visitor, but he hadn't. Bearing in mind the message that she brought, I said I would be delighted.

John asked me this morning at what point I would finish my story – well this is it. The answer came in a way that I certainly did not anticipate. I don't know quite what I am destined to do, or how to go about it, but I now believe that I am on the threshold of something new, and it seems that others do too. My journey continues....

Eighteen – Closing Thoughts

I have faced many challenges, as we all do, but living with Jonathan's death is the biggest challenge I have ever faced. I have needed to call on all the resources at my disposal, and when I think back I can see that over the last four years my experiences have been the preparation. It was since then that I made a conscious choice to develop all aspects of mind, body and spirit, and this has served me well.

As a professional life coach I work with clients who have challenges, and I have thought about how I have developed my own thinking, and how this has helped me to deal with Jonathan's death. I have said to many people that life coaching is not about the past, as it cannot be changed, it is about creating a different future. These words have rung through my head. I do see each day as the start of the rest of my life.

I have been able to make good use of a favourite life coaching question – how do you eat an elephant? Answer - one chunk at a time. This is a reminder that the only way to avoid overwhelm is to take things step by step, and over the last few months this has been an essential approach.

I have thought about the unhelpful nature of 'Why?' questions and how they generate blame and guilt. We have all asked ourselves why we didn't take some action, so that things turned out differently. There is no answer, and I know that allowing this type of questioning to flood your mind can serve no purpose; it is destructive.

I have experienced the impact of freedom of choice and in this case the dreadful effects. The driver made his choice, as did everyone else including Jonathan as he chose that moment to take his final step. Like everyone else, I have a choice as to how to go forward. I have the rest of my life to live with this, and will take my precious memories with me, but I also still have the choice to live my life to the full.

I have demonstrated to myself that even in these circumstances you can choose to take control of your own thoughts - the alternative is to allow your mind to run free. I can recognise when I am heading for a negative spiral of thought, and this awareness has helped me tremendously. This is not avoiding facing the situation, but is about replacing negative thoughts with something more empowering. When you think about it, your own thoughts are the only thing in life over which you actually have control.

As a life coach I was trained to be non-judgemental; to allow people their own way of thinking, acknowledging that they have their reasons, without imposing mine. I have been able to use this to understand the variety of ways in which others have treated me. I accept that some people do not know how to respond, but I don't want advice, I just need people to listen. One of the most difficult things to deal with has been people telling me that I am doomed to many difficult years ahead. They may be right, but I don't need to hear it.

I know that solutions to problems ultimately come from within my own head. Strange though it is, searching for answers is not the way forward; it is much more useful to search for the right question. As a life coach, I ask many questions and the most useful question I have been able to ask myself is – 'if twenty years ago, I had been offered Jonathan for nineteen years or not at all, what would I have said?' There is no doubt over my answer, which makes me realise that the immense pleasure of sharing life with him was my privilege.

Working at my own personal development through coaching over the last few years has helped me tremendously, and similarly the efforts put in to being more physically fit have paid dividends. John and I have wondered how we would have coped if we had been dealing with the physical struggles of a few years ago. Despite the initial daily trips to Manchester we kept on with our jogging, our diet and our different lifestyle. It never crossed my mind that I might need an alcoholic drink until someone offered me one, and it wasn't difficult to decline.

Not taking Paracetamol and various other over-the-counter drugs has enabled me to know exactly how I feel. I have learned to listen to what my body is telling me and try not to ignore it. If I feel tired I rest, if I have a headache I go and drink some water, and I don't immediately turn to the medicine drawer or take something to keep me going. I have learned this lesson once in a way that I will not forget. If I had felt unable to cope over the last eleven weeks, of course I would have gone to the doctors, but up to now I haven't felt any need to. I can only put this down to developing and respecting my physical health.

Although important, no amount of mental or physical preparation could have been as valuable to me as finding a spiritual path. I have learned many things on this journey of faith.

My belief in the importance of a spiritual dimension has been supported by so many events in my life that although logic might tell me otherwise, I know this to be true. Knowing that this world is a temporary diversion from my true being as an eternal spirit has given me a way of dealing with Jonathan's death. I can venture into this other state of consciousness and find that 'peace which passes all understanding' that I recognised four years ago. I can stay there and take the time I need, and it is where I can really be near to God and to Jonathan.

I have become well aware of my ego, and know that it firmly belongs in the earthly world. Ego gives us ideas of power and status and it convinces us that these things will lead us to where we want to be. It is difficult to see through its persuasive power, but as I have become more familiar with the spiritual world, I have realised that ego can actually be put to one side, not that I can always do it.

I have been able to rely upon intuition with a certainty that I know that if I follow my heart, this guidance from God will enable me to do the right thing, to make the right decisions, to say the right things at the right time. In practising this over the last eleven weeks, it has been a revelation to me of the real practical application of my faith. I have allowed myself to be led, and through doing this many things have happened which have been able to reassure me.

As I look back I can see how so many events which at first seem unrelated, are not random but part of the order of things, and have given me the necessary experiences to be able to develop spiritually. As an individual I did not want some of these experiences, but believe that it is the only way that it is possible to have real understanding. I have no doubt that Jonathan fulfilled God's purpose, and that through this everyone involved takes another step toward fulfilling theirs.

My belief that God is Love, that love is the energy that binds us all, and that love is all that really matters has given me a basis on which to live my life. Of course this is what the teachings of Jesus are all about. All my decisions and thoughts can come from this understanding, which I believe is why I feel no need to be angry or bitter about Jonathan's death. I have been told that anger will surface, but it is not there.

I would be the first person to encourage someone to go and learn what they can, but there is a point at which you realise that there is only so much to be learned from the experiences of others, and that a journey of spiritual learning is something that you have to travel on your own. When you look quietly inside, you find that you know what you need to know, that it was there all along. However, the willingness to embark on this journey is not for the half hearted. If you open that door to God through Jesus, and leave the safety chain on, the benefits will be limited. To begin this journey, either you decide to surrender and invite your guide right in, or you don't really get going. It will change your life, and it's natural to be scared about where that might lead, but my experience has given me such inner strength that I can't think why anyone would want to turn this offer down.

People all over the world are waking up to the idea that there is, as the saying goes, 'more to life than meets the eye' and that true spiritual growth leads to peace and love which, whatever our beliefs, is where we all want to head. This is not something that is available just to the educated or wealthy, it is available to everyone. I don't cease to be amazed by the fact that so many people are coming to the same general conclusion, in spite of such differing backgrounds. I consider myself very fortunate that John's self-employment has allowed me the freedom of time to explore without the pressure to earn an income, and that I have made such progress. Of course, there's no prize attached to the speed of your spiritual journey, what counts is that you make a start and then keep going.

In the circles in which I move, people do not talk about their spiritual beliefs, and although meditation is mentioned and occasionally God, Christianity is rather unfashionable. Four years ago, I had what I can only describe as a brief spiritual encounter which was so powerful that it changed my way of thinking about God, and made me want to investigate further. Many people these days search and find a connection to God and, with or without following a specific faith, are able to use the peace that this brings to their everyday life. My journey of faith started off like this, but I knew I had further to go, and my faith in God led me to Christianity. In some ways it is much simpler just to accept that God will guide us all if we just tune ourselves in, and I had, but in the end I couldn't ignore Jesus. In terms of historical proof, what we know about the life of Jesus has been verified beyond doubt. However, he didn't just claim to have found God or even the route to God, he said he was effectively God – the way, the truth and the life.

Most people come to Christianity by learning about Jesus and then finding their route to God, but I didn't. I looked from the opposite perspective, and concluded that if you know God, then everything about Jesus becomes consistent with what you might expect God to be in human terms. From humble beginnings, Jesus was able to explain difficult spiritual concepts through stories, which made them understandable at the level where the individual could find meaning. He found the answers within the stillness of himself, where he could connect with his spiritual side through meditation and prayer. He was able to do things that scientifically we cannot explain; we can only call them miracles. He knew that there was an order to events and that his future would unfold accordingly. He knew that love was the basis of everything and is really all that matters, and his message was simple – 'love God and love your neighbour'. When he died he demonstrated that the spirit in life is eternal, by reappearing not just to one person but to hundreds and on different occasions. After his death his followers recognised a power that they could know as a guide called the Holy Spirit, which allowed them to maintain their own relationship with God, as Jesus had promised.

These days people spend fortunes on all manner of courses, books and advisors trying to find a route to peace and happiness. The fact is that the answers to what so many people are looking for are not in the earthly world around us, the answers ultimately are found in the spiritual world, which can only be accessed from within. The amazing thing is that the guidance you need to attain these things was made available nearly two thousand years ago and it is free, yet most people still choose to ignore it. In the world in which we live, it is not just some inner fulfilment that people are searching for, but also support through the everyday challenges of life, and through Christianity I have found both of these. If your spirituality takes you down the road of the enlightened recluse, that's fine. But for most us, life is about being part of the world, and in Jesus we have been given the perfect guide because he didn't just talk about it, he lived it.

It seems to me that belief in God, being a Christian, and supporting one of the branches of organised religion like the Church of England can be practised together or quite independently. My route from the Alpha course took me to our local church, not because it was suggested, but because I wanted to go. It happened to be the Church of England, which many people, both members and non-members, see as an outdated, rigid structure in much need of change. The politics of the particular Church denomination make no difference to me, as I believe it all comes back to the same fundamental truths in the end. Whatever view you take, it remains a focal point for people coming together. It is a place that you can regularly renew your spiritual beliefs, and it is necessary to find a way to do this constantly, if you want to keep them in sight when surrounded by all the pressures of this world. Knowing that there is a structure outside of yourself, to which you can turn, is very important whatever form that takes, otherwise the spiritual path would be quite lonely. When Jonathan died the Church was the only place that I wanted to go.

I certainly don't think that I have all the answers, no one has, but I have learned such a lot and I am still learning. I think of God like my mobile phone, Christianity as my network provider. I can't explain how it works. I press the right buttons and make a connection. In fact it really doesn't matter to me how it works, I don't need the explanation or the theory. It is the very experience of connecting that makes it real for me.

Life is not about doing or having, although these are the processes through which we create our future and learn our lessons, it is about being with God. Our ultimate life purpose is to reconnect with God. In life coaching, it has been my privilege to act as a guide and help people to achieve their earthly goals, and I intend to continue to do this. However, I believe it is an even greater privilege to work with individuals and help them to find God, not by imposing belief but by facilitating their personal journey.

If each human soul is to find what it is searching for, and the world is going to be a peaceful place, it is not going to happen by tackling the external symptoms of how we live. The place to start is within each individual, with each of us encompassing the spiritual journey that is our birthright. I believe this will happen as people find God through a faith to which they can relate, and one that they can see will support them in their lives. It is not the world that we need to go and change – it is us.

Nineteen - One Year On

Although I have carried much sadness through this last year, I am also aware that it has been a year of many interesting insights and wonderful opportunities. When I started writing 'Baring My Soul', I didn't really know whether it was simply a way for me to unload my emotions. I had no idea where my writing might lead, but I did sense that one day my efforts would be read by others. Last summer, somewhat tentatively and nervously I gave my manuscript to a few close family members and friends to read, and waited for some feedback. The response I had in phone calls, letters and emails could best be summed up as one of gratitude, and encouragement to investigate publication.

Although we are not necessarily aware of the effect, every choice and every event changes our lives. Some seem insignificant and remain so, others seem insignificant at the time and then when you look back you realise their tremendous importance, and others have a huge and immediate impact. I was already aware of my journey of faith, but what occurred when Jonathan died and in the last year has had an enormous impact. My journal since then is filled with many discoveries, adventures into prayer, being introduced to some amazing people, reading some incredible books, some remarkable 'coincidences', doing things that I never thought I would do, including speaking at the Shropshire Prayer Breakfast and organising a Christian meditation group, and even pheasants. Maybe these stories will be the introductory chapters to another book!

One of the first people to read 'Baring My Soul' was a coaching colleague's wife who shared with me some information on a course in Spiritual Direction that she had applied to attend in London, and in which she thought I might be interested. I also attended an 'away day' for our local churches and listened with great interest to a lady who described herself as a Prayer Guide. Following Jonathan's funeral, I met up with an old friend, now ordained, for an afternoon cup of tea, and a few days later she sent a paper cutting from the Church Times which dropped through the letterbox with the details of a new course at the University of Wales, Lampeter on Spiritual Direction. Les, our vicar, read my book and returned it with several flyers about Spirituality courses in the Diocese, and also asked me if I might like to be a part of the local ministry team.

Last year, in the closing thoughts of my book I wrote 'in life coaching it has been my privilege to act as a guide and help people to achieve their earthly goals, and I intend to continue to do this. However, I believe it is an even greater privilege to work with individuals and help them to find God, not by imposing belief but by facilitating their personal journey'. When I wrote these words I had never heard of Spiritual Direction, but soon realised that the combination of Spiritual Direction and Life Coaching is exactly what I was describing. I attended the course at Lampeter, and am currently attending the Spirituality and Prayer Guide course run by the Lichfield Diocese, and have no doubt that this is where my future lies.

Through my life coaching, I know that there is tremendous demand from individuals from all walks of life to understand themselves, to understand how they fit in to the world, to uncover their life purpose, to find inner peace, to know God, and to be at one with all things. These answers can be a struggle to find by yourself – it is unknown territory and it can be scary. Equally these topics can be extremely difficult to share with others, as for most of us they are challenging even to talk about. The sea of life can be very choppy, but when you remain on the surface at least you have the security that you can see the waves coming. If you go deep enough beneath the surface then it will be calm, but you don't know what surprises might be there. Taking this plunge into your inner life with a spiritual companion who is non-judgmental, non advisory, non directive and open minded seems to me to be something that could be of tremendous value to many individuals.

As I continue on my journey the more clear it becomes to me that there is only one God, that God is love, that religions are expressions of this God, and that despite the differences in beliefs there is a level at which we do all come together as one. In learning to move toward this place, the answers that so many people are searching for are revealed. They cannot be found in a textbook or on a course; they come from within. It was back in 2001 after my confirmation that I realised that to make progress on this journey I needed not just to be able to theorise about, but to experience communion with God, and that this could only be achieved through personal prayer. At that time I didn't really know how to start, and my only concept of prayer was through words. I now realise that not only can words be used in many ways, but also that prayer can take many forms of visualisation, creativity, beauty, feelings, meditation and so on.

The importance of developing the spiritual side of our humanity has been buried for many of us under the demands and pressures of society, but it is the natural state of being. It transcends religious belief, but it is religious teaching that has helped many millions of people to understand and make this journey throughout the centuries. The challenge for each of us as individuals is to find the way that is right for us, to become aware of God in our lives, and to find forms of everyday prayer that take us forward on our spiritual journey.

In February 2002 I wrote in my journal, 'I know that through the coaching somehow combined with Christianity wonderful things will happen'. I shared these words in 2003 in writing Chapter Nine of this book, and now in 2004 they feel even more true. The events of the last few years keep pointing me in the same direction and although it would be very much easier for me to ignore, I really can't ignore the magnetic effect of this inner compass. To use the skills, knowledge and experience that I have been given over the past few years to help others on their spiritual journey, is what I know I have to do. Looking back, I think I have probably always known this, but could not have verbalised it, and would not have had a clue how to start. It seems now that paths are opening up, and although I don't know the exact nature or timing, it simply doesn't matter. My experiences of the last few years suggest that I don't need the details of the plan at present, or the precise goal. All I need to do is to keep developing my relationship with God, in the confidence that the guidance I need will come.

Bibliography

1. Awaken the Giant Within – Anthony Robbins (1991) Simon & Schuster

2. Questions of Life – Nicky Gumbel (1993) – Kingsway Publications

3. Co-Active Coaching - Whitworth, Kimsey-House & Sandahl (1998) – Davies-Black

4. Into the Light – (1997) – British and Foreign Bible Society

5. Conversations with God – Book 1 – Neale Donald Walsch (1997) – Hodder & Stoughton

6. Every Day with Jesus - Selwyn Hughes & Philip Greenslade – CWR

7. Thirsting For God - Audio Tape – Nightingale Conant

8. The Prophet – Kahlil Gibran (1998) – Oneworld Publications

9. Find it fast in the Bible – Ron Rhodes (2000) – Harvest House

10. From Black and White to Colour – Richard Wilkins (1999) Cantecia

11. How to know God - Deepak Chopra (2000) - Rider

This book was written to raise awareness of the spiritual journey that is there for us all. I hope that wherever you are, my words may provide some enlightenment, hope, and encouragement, but more than that be an inspiration to you to keep going.

Any profit from this publication will be put into a fund to help individuals make progress on their spiritual journey, through personal support, group workshops and any other ways that could encourage individual spiritual growth.

If you would like to share your thoughts with me, think I might be able to help you in any way, or if you want to purchase additional copies of this book, I can be contacted by post, email or telephone as follows.

Julie Roberts
Longacre House,
Wilcott,
Nesscliffe,
Shrewsbury
SY4 1BJ

0845 458 1077

julie@goingsolo.net

Printed in the United Kingdom
by Lightning Source UK Ltd.
113105UKS00001B/361